Thomas Holcroft, Isabelle Montolieu

Caroline of Lichtfield

A Novel. Second Edition. Vol. II

Thomas Holcroft, Isabelle Montolieu

Caroline of Lichtfield

A Novel. Second Edition. Vol. II

ISBN/EAN: 9783337004217

Printed in Europe, USA, Canada, Australia, Japan

Cover: Foto ©Thomas Meinert / pixelio.de

More available books at **www.hansebooks.com**

CAROLINE

OF

LICHTFIELD.

CAROLINE

OF

LICHTFIELD;

A NOVEL.

TRANSLATED FROM THE FRENCH.

By THOMAS HOLCROFT.

Idole d'un cœur juſte, & paſſion du Sage,
Amitié, que ton nom foutienne cet ouvrage ;
Règne dans mes écrits, ainſi que dans mon cœur,
Tu m'appris à connoître, à fentir, le bonheur.
VOLTAIRE.

THE SECOND EDITION.

VOL. III.

LONDON:

PRINTED FOR G. G. J. AND J. ROBINSON,
PATERNOSTER - ROW.
M DCC LXXXVI.

CAROLINE

OF

LICHTFIELD.

....

THESE two letters being sent, and
thus being more tranquil, relative
to the fate of Matilda, the Count applied
himself wholly to the plan he had formed,
in order to ascertain the happiness of
Caroline. He had desired the High Cham-

berlain to come to Ronebourg, fo foon as his daughter fhould be informed of the death of the Baronefs. It could not be long before Lindorf muſt arrive, and the Count was determined to fet off for Berlin the moment he came; pretending to have received an order from the King, and to leave Lindorf at Ronebourg, with the High Chamberlain, that he might obtain a divorce from his Majeſty, and his con‑ fent, alſo, for the marriage of Lindorf and Caroline. He then intended to write and inform them of their happinefs; and, without feeing them, to depart for Drefden. From Drefden, he meant to go to Eng‑ land with Matilda; or without her, if fhe determined to marry the young Baron de Zaftrow; and to refide there with his mother's relations. He felt fufficient for‑ titude to make Caroline and his friend happy, but not to be a daily witnefs of their loves; and this plan, once fixed, he held to be unalterable.

Alas! he knew not yet all the power of love; had yet not felt all its vengeful effects. The more he ftruggled with paf-fion the deeper was it rooted in his heart. How often, when befide Caroline, unable to reftrain his feelings, was he ready to kneel at her feet, confefs his affection, his internal ftruggles, his defpair; appeal to her generofity, recall to mind the facred bond by which they were united, the vows they had mutually made, and employ every refource, of pity and of paffion, in fupplicating her confent to live and die with the hufband by whom fhe was adored. By flight only could he obtain a victory over himfelf, on thefe occafions. Once

B 2   out

out of her fight, and virtue, delicacy, and friendfhip, again were afcendant. Love ceded to duty ; and he had the fortitude to imagine Caroline in the arms of another, and not expire at the thought ! Then would he remember Lindorf, banifhed from his country, dragging an unhappy being through foreign climates, deprived of his miftrefs and his friend, without confolation and without hope; and, re-membering, fhudder and deteft his weak-nefs : again renew his oaths to fubdue it, and, fearing to expofe himfelf to future dangers, deprive himfelf of the pleafure of feeing Caroline ; who, ill interpreting the caufe of his abfence, would, on her part, weep and afflict herfelf at conduct which fhe fuppofed to be the moft une-quivocal proof of indifference.

In

'In her moments of vexation and defpair, fhe ftrengthened herfelf in the
refolution of returning to Rindaw, and of
entreating, nay, of abfolutely requiring his
confent, fhould he offer any oppofition.
"Alas!" would fhe reply to this doubt,
"far from oppofing, he will gladly feize the
means of living feparate from Caroline.—
Separate!—What! am I no more to fee
him, to hear him no more? And, when I
quit this place, muft a lafting feparation
enfue? And muft I afk it; muft I myfelf
pronounce the fatal fentence? No! never
fhall I acquire force adequate to a tafk
like this! When he fhall have the cruelty
to command, fubmiffion will furely be
fufficient punifhment."

Yet did her friendfhip for the Baronefs,
at fome moments, make her even defire this

fepa-

feparation, and vanquifh her fears of quitting Walftein. The High Chamberlain,
as had been concerted with the Count,
endeavoured to prepare her to fupport the
death of her friend. In his firft letters,
he fpoke of remedies fhe had taken, to
recover her fight, which were powerful and
fomewhat dangerous. He afterwards wrote
word her blindnefs was paft cure, and
that it afflicted her fo much fhe had fallen
ill. Caroline no fooner heard this than
fhe wifhed to fly to attend and confole
her; but fhe herfelf was yet too feeble for
the fatigues of fuch a journey. She wrote
the moft affecting letters, both to her friend
and her father; and, every returning courier,
hoped to hear of her recovery. At length
the letters of the High Chamberlain became fo alarming, and affirmed fo pofi-
tively

tively the Baronefs of Rindaw was in the
utmoft danger, that Caroline immediately
determined to fet off; and fent to beg the
Count would come and fpeak with her.

He found her with her eyes fwimming
in tears, and well divined their caufe.—
" O ! Sir," faid fhe, the moment he entered,
" read here what my father has written !
My dear Mamma is very, very ill; nay,
perhaps worfe than he fays. Let me intreat you to give immediate orders for
my departure; for I will inftantly be gone
to Rindaw. Never fhall I forgive myfelf
for having delayed fo long. Should I be
too late, fhould I never more behold the
tendereft, deareft of friends——"

The Count, finding this idea had
prefented itfelf to her mind, and that the

appre-

apprehenfion had had half its effect, thought this the time to inform her of the truth: befide that her refolution to depart immediately, made fecrefy any longer impoffible.——" Dear Caroline," faid he, feating himfelf befide her, and taking one of her hands, " let me intreat you, in the name of Heaven, to be calm; think of the injury you may do yourfelf ! Scarcely recovered from a moft dangerous illnefs, can you fuftain——"

" Yes any thing, every thing ! It is my duty to devote my returning ftrength to the fervice of the friend who has been, to me, the beft and tendereft of mothers. I feel how much I have neglected this duty, and fhall, indeed, be moft happy, may I but have the means to repair my wrongs."

She

She was going to rife and make preparations, but the Count again detained her.
" A moment, dear Caroline, be appeafed
for a moment, I conjure you, and liften to
me——I have alfo received a letter from
your father."

" Merciful God!" cried fhe, turning pale,
and prefaging what was coming; " a letter
to you! Tell me! I beg you, inftantly,
tell me its contents. Has my father
concealed any thing ?—Oh ! Sir,—" Her
oppreffed heart could no longer refift the
violence of agitation, and her fobs interrupted fpeech. The filence of the
Count, his downcaft eyes, the timid compaffion of his countenance, and the vague
anfwers he returned, confirmed her fears,
and her defpair became exceffive. "Oh God!
Oh God!" exclaimed fhe, " I perceive, I

perceive

perceive I no longer have a friend, no longer have any thing in this world! My dear Mamma no longer exifts, and I have loft my all!"

" Not fo, dear Caroline; there ftill is a friend in the world, who hopes to prove how dear you are to him, and how much he is interefted in your happinefs."

Caroline loved this friend too well herfelf to be wholly infenfible of that confolation he wifhed to impart; and to thofe new proofs of tendernefs which fhe no longer had dared to hope. Her tears ftill flowed, abundantly flowed, but lefs bitterly. In the affaults of violent grief, the feeling and impaffioned mind experiences relief by the company of a beloved object, and in the alleviations of love. She grieved, but the Count grieved with her, felt as fhe felt,

and

and partook of her affliction. In thefe their moments of melancholy, their fouls were in unifon. Caroline had loft the tendereft of friends, but the very moment in which fhe was informed of this misfortune was that which gave her the fweet hope of being beloved, by the hufband fhe adored ; for, in this firft tranfport of defpair, which foftened fortitude and fhewed Caroline ftill more lovely, the Count was not able wholly to reprefs his paffion. The forrow of Caroline demanded every care and confolation friendfhip could afford ; and Walftein, while he endeavoured to affume the form of friendfhip, had all the tendereft actions and looks of love. Caroline, thus, in the midft of affliction, had a glimpfe of a happy futurity, and mourned that her friend was not to be a witnefs of her blifs.

She defired to be informed, circumftanti-
ally, of her illnefs and death; but the Count,
who underftood nothing fo ill as diffimulation, referred her to the High Chamberlain, who would foon return ; yet, to quiet
her remorfe for having too long delayed going to the aid of her friend, he told her fhe
had died fome time fince, and when it was
impoffible for Caroline to have gone to her
affiftance. No fooner was the High Chamberlain informed that his daughter knew
the truth than he returned to Ronebourg,
and told her, himfelf, fhe was left fole
heirefs to the Canonefs. She had made
her will anew, after fhe had been informed
of her marriage, and it was to the Countefs
of Walftein fhe had bequeathed all her pof-
feffions : fhe had indeed left a legacy to the
Count, purpofely, as fhe herfelf had word-

ed

ed it, to prove how highly she was satisfied
at his union with Caroline. She recommended, in most affecting terms, the happiness of this her beloved pupil, to Walstein ; and to Caroline that of the best and
most sublime of men.

The reading of the will drew many tears
from Caroline ; nor was the Count less affected. The High Chamberlain, alone,
read it with perfect satisfaction, and com-
prehended not how an augmentation of fortune could become the subject of sorrow.
Caroline, alas! found only new motives, in
these benefactions, to regret a friend so
tender and so generous. Walstein, dif-
tracted by a thousand contrary sensations,
could not hear of union and happiness,
which he so soon was to renounce, without
extreme emotion. When the Baron came

to that article, he fuddenly kneeled to Caroline; "yes," faid he, with vehement tranfport, "yes, by honour, by love, by every thing facred I fwear, you fhall be happy, Caroline."—He could not continue; and Caroline, affected to excefs, tenderly ftretched out her hand to raife him, while fhe felt, more powerfully than ever, that on him, only, of all the world, this her promifed happinefs depended, and on the fentiments he fhould entertain for her.

Had they been alone, perhaps, fhe might then have told him what hers really were; perhaps this might have been the happy moment of an explanation too long delayed; but the prefence of the placid High Chamberlain checked fuch effufions of the heart. He, with wonderful tranquillity, continued to read the will; which contained

ed nothing farther, except legacies to fervants and vaffals. The Count, unable to
fupport the continuance of his prefent
emotion and the tears of the compaffionate
Caroline, left the room and walked into the
park, whither all his feelings went with him.
He began no longer to underftand his own
proceedings; and, fometimes, afked himfelf
wherefore he thus fhould wilfully be for
ever miferable. Wherefore fhould he yield
the poffeffion of her on whom he had fo
many claims, and without whom it was impoffible to live? " She begins," thought he,
" to be accuftomed to me; nay I even think
I behold expreffions of affection in her eyes.
Alas! I know it can be but friendfhip,
efteem, gratitude; yet may not thefe fenfations, in a mind like hers, well fupply
the place of love? Or may I ever hope to
infpire others? Does fhe not already grant

more

more than I could ever expect ? But, while I know, paft doubt, her heart wholly appertains to another, to Lindorf!—Lindorf? Alas ! perhaps he no longer is in exiftence ; perhaps he has fallen a victim to a paffion the effects of which I have every caufe to fear ; perhaps he has funk under his grief, under the grief of Caroline, by which my own heart has been fo often wounded, and which muft be renewed, with fuch excefs, fhould fhe hear tidings fo fatal !

The Count fhuddered while he imagined he himfelf might be the meffenger to inform Caroline of the death of the man fhe loved ; that he himfelf muft then be confidered as the caufe of his death.. The filence of Lindorf, after the fhort letter he could not but have received, appeared to him a certain proof his fears were but too well founded ;

founded ; and fo much did this and fuck like fears torment him that fcarcely could reafon fuftain the conflicts of the heart. At one moment he would paffionately wifh the return of Lindorf, and dread it worfe than death the next; equally fearing to fee him arrive or to hear he was no longer in exiftence. Thus did a man fo philofophic, fo fage, fo wholly, till then, mafter of himfelf, at length, feel the empire of paffion and its tyrannic power; and, while thus he felt, terrified at its effects, again he fwore to vanquifh it, to devote himfelf, if it were not too late, to the felicity of thofe he loved.

From one of thefe tormenting terrors he was, at laft, relieved. He received a lettey from Varner, the valet de chambre of Lindorf, to whom he had given his fhort and

and preffing letter, written to conjure his friend to return. " The good Varner en-
" treated his Excellency not to be uneafy
" at not having yet received an anfwer to
" this letter, for that, when he came to
" Hamburg, his mafter was not there; he
" had embarked, a few days before, for
" England, with a Saxon gentleman; and
" he, Varner, detained three weeks at
" Hamburg by contrary winds, had neither
" been able to join his mafter, who ex-
" pected him at London, nor, confequent-
" ly, to remit him the letter his Excellen-
" cy had confided to his care."

The firft pleafure of the Count was to learn that Lindorf ftill lived, and, by be-ing able to travel, was in good health. Nor was this pleafure fingle; Lindorf had not received his letter, his return was there-

fore

fore deferred, and this fhort delay, which likewife deferred the moment when Wal-ftein fhould be obliged to quit Caroline, cede her to another, and live for ever from her, was to him an age of happinefs. He haftened therefore to her chamber, that he might not lofe moments fo precious. Her father was with her. "My dear Count," faid the High Chamberlain, as Walftein enter-ed, "my daughter, here, is exceedingly defirous of quitting Ronebourg, but dares not fpeak to you on the fubject. For my part, I can fee no reafon in the world why you fhould remain longer here; for, at prefent, the Countefs is fufficiently recover-ed to undertake the journey. The King may complain of your long abfence; he com-manded me to haften your return to Ber-lin, and in a tone that will not admit of longer delay. I muft certainly be gone;

for

for my prefence is abfolutely neceffary at court. If, therefore, your Excellency fhall think proper to give orders, we will incontinently depart together."

The Count made no reply, but fixed his eyes on Caroline, in order to inquire of her countenance what was paffing in her heart, and whether fhe really wifhed to leave Ronebourg. Caroline blufhed, look-ed down, and, by her filence, feemed to approve. Yet was the embarraffment of the Count beyond defcription great. He could not be ignorant how much the King defired his return; for, fince his arrival from Ruffia, he had only remained four and twenty hours at Berlin; and had had but one fhort interview with his Majefty. To the friendfhip of the Sovereign, only, was he indebted for his prefent long abfence; and frequent couriers brought him pref-

fing

fing letters from the King; or rather from a man who reclaimed his friend. Walftein knew, likewife, that his marriage with Caroline was then become public. The High Chamberlain, who fo long had laboured with this fecret, had told it the whole world, as foon as his daughter was gone to Ronebourg. The King himfelf, knowing the Count and Countefs were together, had openly fpoken of their union; wherefore longer myftery was impoffible. Yet how might the Count, with his prefent intentions, take Caroline to Berlin as the Countefs of Walftein, and there prefent her at court, and to every body, by a name fhe fo foon was to quit?

He then felt how much the delay of his letter to Lindorf deranged all his projects. He no longer could refufe the requeft of the King, which might every moment be

changed

changed to a command ; he could not think of leaving Caroline, alone, at Ronebourg ; and ftill lefs of taking her to Rindaw, where every thing muft tend to nourifh and increafe affliction. While reflecting, in this dilemma, how he muft act, Caroline, preffed by her fatner to confirm her defire to depart immediately, faid, "fhe fhould, with pleafure, accompany my Lord the Count to Berlin ; but that fhe hoped both he and the King would have the goodnefs, for fome time, to difpenfe with her feeing company ; and that, while fhe remained in mourning, fhe might be permitted to live retired."

Walftein eagerly caught the idea ; and the health of Caroline, not yet fufficiently re-eftablifhed, together with her deep mourning for a friend whom fhe had loved

as

as a mother, were, in reality, excellent
pretexts for complying with her request,
and neither receiving nor paying vifits, at
Berlin, for fome months. In lefs time
than that Walftein well might hope his
future fate would be decided. Caroline,
mean while, would live almoft unknown,
at Walftein-houfe, where fhe would fee
only her father, and himfelf; which, to him,
was a moft pleafing reflection. It was
fome alleviation to defpair not to be
obliged to quit her before the dreaded
hour of final feparation fhould arrive.
The fage in love is but a man. The
Count no longer faw impediments. Caroline living in his houfe, and in his fight,
was perfection of blifs ; and, though he
ftill deftined her for a man he fuppofed
fhe loved, though ftill determined carefully to conceal his own paffion, he could

not

not refuse himself this intermediate enjoy-
ment of happiness; which, beside, would
remove every difficulty, relative to where
Caroline should remain.

The day of departure was, therefore,
fixed; and the tender Caroline beheld it
arrive with rapture. She should no longer
live in the mansion of Lindorf: it was
now determined she should for ever pass
her life with the husband she adored: and
she thought herself certain of soon effacing
from his memory, by offices of tender
affection, the capricious and erroneous
conduct which her heart, at present, dif-
claimed; and which she herself could
never pardon. Walstein, attentive to every
action and look of Caroline, perceived she
went with pleasure; but this pleasure he
ascribed to virtue, and to the desire she

had,

had, henceforth, of avoiding every thing that might bring Lindorf to memory. His esteem, consequently, his affection, were redoubled; but, thinking thus, he was but the more strongly confirmed in his determination of rewarding the virtue he so much admired.

Behold them, then, at Berlin, and alighting at Walstein-house; a place of so much former terror to Caroline. She entered it with all those gentle sensations, those mild hopes, so sweet to the soul, and which seemed a prelude of the felicity she was about to enjoy. To these succeeded the recollection of her bridal day; her behaviour to the man she now adored, the mixture of hope and fear concerning the real sentiments of the Count, and the melancholy reflection on the death of her dear friend,

Vol. III. C whom

whom she wished a witness of her present happiness. These, all conspiring, contributed but to augment that emotion which she no longer could conceal, and which brought the tears into her eyes. The Count saw those tears; his heart melted at the sight; he attributed them to a very different cause, and would instantly have given her every assurance that cause should be removed; but we have before seen the motives by which he was withheld. He would not give her a prospect of bliss as yet uncertain; nor would he have to combat with her delicacy and generosity. Neither, indeed, had he the power to pronounce *I yield Caroline to another*. No, he might have acted; but, on such a subject, he could not have spoken!

The

The High Chamberlain supped with them, and retired inflate with joy, at beholding his daughter now eftablished Lady of Walftein-houfe. When he was gone, the Count led Caroline to the apartment which long had been deftined to receive her; at the time of his marriage, and while he was far from prefaging the events that were to fucceed. He had furnished it with all poffible tafte and magnificence, in the dear expectation that his young and beauteous bride was foon to become its inhabitant. This expectation, at laft, was realized. But how? In what manner? And at what moment? How much might he well regret paft fufpence, and the hope which, during uncertainty, he had cherished!

This

" This, dear Caroline," faid he, as they entered, " is the apartment which has long been referved for you." Caroline, who fuppofed a latent reproach was lurking in thefe few words, looked down, and alternately blufhed and turned pale. Walftein faw this, but faw not the true motive. Eager to deprive her of her fears, " you," faid he, refpectfully kiffing her hand, " are abfolute here; queen of this apartment, neither I nor any one elfe fhall enter it, without your free permiffion."

Haftily the Count retired; had he remained a moment longer, he, perhaps, had forgotten Lindorf and all his oaths— " Ye powers of friendfhip !" cried he, as he entered his own chamber, " fuftain my fortitude. Caroline, dear adored Caroline, Lindorf, my friend, appear, be ever prefent sent to my imagination, there inceffantly repeat.you cannot be happy afunder.!"

Thus did the whole night pass in mourning over and lamenting his destiny, and the rigid sacrifice which virtue, principle, friendship, and even love itself, loudly demanded. Caroline, though more tranquil, yet slept but little and reflected much. Though her chaste simplicity felt not all the singularity of Walstein's conduct, yet could she not be wholly ignorant that her spouse had a right to partake of her apartment; she thought the wrongs she had done him too many, and too great, not to attribute his leaving her thus to well-founded resentment. Succeeding evenings but confirmed the idea; Walstein, fearing again to encounter dangers he found himself so near sinking under before, not only forbore to

accompany

accompany Caroline to her apartment but began, as he had done at Ronebourg, before she knew the death of the Baroness, to abfent himfelf as much as poffible, and never be with her, except in the prefence of her father, or her women; and even then he had an air of conftraint, of anxiety, fo vifible, he feared fo much to meet her eyes, or to approach her touch, that she no longer doubted of his indifference; nay, she even dreaded it was averfion. This conduct, far from irritating, fenfibly affected Caroline. Herfelf, alone, and her former caprice did she accufe. Perhaps he fought to punifh them, and he had good right; or, rather, her unjuft flight, and the diflike she fo long had teftified, had at length wholly incurred his hatred. Yet his tender and continued cares, his mild and gentle attentions dur-

ing

ing her illnefs, and her grief, what were they?—Generofity, natural benevolence, fympathy, compaffion; which ever are inherent in the noble mind. But fhe too plainly faw, at prefent, the chains by which he was reftrained were become deteftable; yes, he groaned over that fatality by which they had been united. She recollected his travelling defign, and doubted not but he ftill intended it fhould take place; fhe even, for a moment, thought to prevent his being again at the pain of propofing her return to Rindaw; and thus, by vo- luntarily abfenting herfelf from the Count and the court, reftore him the liberty of which fhe thought him fo ardently defirous. But this propofal was become much more difficult to execute than when fhe wrote her letter at Rindaw. At prefent fhe loved him, paffionately loved him; and

C 4   never

never could she collect the fortitude to
abandon the object of this her most tender
affection. Therefore, her design was no
sooner formed than forsaken; and to that
succeeded the resolution to try all possible
means of regaining the heart of her hufband, and, by love, obliterating the remembrance of former wrongs. While she
meditated she hoped. "He is so benevolent, has so much sensibility, is so little
inclined to revenge injuries," said she,
"that, when he shall behold how infinitely
I love him, will he refuse to return my
love; or will he not, at least, grant me
his friendship?"

Thus did the noble and sympathetic
heart of Caroline cling to her Walstein;
thus teach her how to estimate his worth;
and thus did hope, with mild and benig-

nant

nant impulfe, bid her feek his fociety with greater affiduity than even he fought to avoid hers. Obfervant of this new ardor, the Count, far from imagining himfelf beloved, attributed all the attentions, all the thoufand kindneffes of Caroline to fyftematic gratitude and duty; which a foul fo feeling, and fo virtuous, as hers, had impofed upon itfelf. Momentary appearances confirmed the fufpicion. Caroline, young and timid, feeling fenfations fhe thought fhe had not the power to communicate, reproaching herfelf for, and even exaggerating former errors, fearing by officioufnefs to difpleafe a hufband prejudiced againft her, often had an air of referve and conftraint, which perfuaded Walftein her heart was acting contrary to its moft ardent defires. Sorrowful at the ill fuccefs of her endeavours to infpire

affection,

affection, often would she suffer melancholy to invade her mind; often would retire to her chamber, and on her lovely cheeks leave traces of tears which the Count imagined to be the bitter tears of duty; shed in lamenting the severity of fate, that separated her from the man she loved.

. Him, day after day did Walstein wait for. Him, the lover and the friend, for whom felicity so supreme was held in reserve; nor could he comprehend wherefore he did not return. Beside the letter he had sent by Varner, he had also written after his arrival at Berlin; and his letter, under cover to, and recommended to the care of Lindorf's banker, at Hamburg, by him to be forwarded to England, must have reached him if he were not already on the road, coming back. This letter

was

was more pressing than the former. Without fully expressing all he meant, he used
every argument to hasten his return. " On
" this his own happiness and the happi-
" ness of those he most loved depended; if
" prayers and entreaties were not sufficient,
" he absolutely exacted a compliance.—
" Recollect, dear Lindorf, how often you
" have given me the right of disposing of
" your future destiny. This right, which
" I hold from friendship, and, perhaps,
" from gratitude somewhat too enthusi-
" astic, I now claim. Yes, I now recall
" to memory every circumstance which
" may make you hold yourself my debtor
" to tell you the hour is come when it
" depends on you to cancel them all,
" and, by one single act, place all obliga-
" tion to my account. I can only add,
" if in a month, at fartheft, I have not the

" pleasure

" pleafure to embrace you, at Walftein-
" houfe, you will give me reafon to doubt
" of an attachment which I think I deferve,
" and. to fuppofe I no longer have a
" friend!"

This letter, fo ftrong, fo preffing, remaining unanfwered, gave room to imagine, and even to believe that, in fact,
Lindorf had fet out for Berlin before it
arrived at England; and that confequent-
ly he muft foon be there. Dreadful as
this moment was, in which a feparation
from her he adored was to take place,
ftill Walftein waited for it with a kind of
impatience, arifing from a conviction it
would afcertain the happinefs of Caroline,
and from a wifh of being himfelf freed
from that incertitude which fuffers the foul
to wander among illufive chimeras, which

an inftant might deftroy, and to which
mifery itfelf is fometimes preferable.

· How, indeed, was he to defend himfelf
againft the phantoms of hope, féductive
and dear as they are to the heart, and whofe
fpells each day became more potent, more
irrefiftible? Nothing, indeed, but the
modefty and prefent error of Walftein could
have prevented him from perceiving they
were not phantoms, were not illufive. Far
from defifting, Caroline was ftill more affectionate, more attentive, mild and tender. The happinefs of her exiftence was
the prize for which fhe contended. And
how might fhe perform too much for a
hufband like Walftein, whom fhe fo long
had offended, by averfion moft unjuft; to
whom her heart had been unfaithful, and
which had fo many errors, nay, to Caroline,

line, crimes to obliterate? Repulfing diffidence, therefore, and hoping every thing from perfeverance and affection, a thoufand kind arts were employed to draw and attach him to her, of which love alone is fufceptible, and to which love alone can give fuch wondrous force.

The Count was exceedingly fond of mufic, and Caroline was inceffant in her endeavours to arrive at excellence. Often did fhe entreat him to accompany her on the flute or violoncello, which he played equally well; often did fhe fing, with all the charms of fenfibility, the moft expreffive and melting airs, and fuch as moft were likely to make impreffion on a foul like Walftein's. The Count had a tafte and talents for drawing, but other occupations had prevented him from making

any

any great progrefs in the art. Caroline,
on the contrary, educated in retirement,
had applied herfelf with infinite fuccefs to
that delightful art, which can people
folitude, and, in defpite of wintry froft,
retrace nature's beauties, create meads,
rivers, mountains, and forefts, and make
permanent the fleeting and perifhing beauties of Flora. Caroline was particularly
fuccefsful in flowers and landfcapes;
which alfo was the fpecies of painting the
Count moft preferred. She offered to in-
ftruct him, direct his effays, and correct
his miftakes; in return for which, fhe entreated him to felect books, and fuperin-
tend ftudies which fhe was defirous to
engage in, but which are too generally neglected in the education of women. While
he was drawing by her fide, fometimes
would fhe read, and her former cuftom of

reading

reading aloud to her dear mamma, added
to the native intelligence and feeling fhe
poffeffed, rendered her indeed a moft excellent reader. Walftein, when he faw
her fatigued, would read in his turn; and
while her countenance, obedient to the
powers of genius, affumed the paffion or
imbibed the wifdom of the writer, her
fkilful and delicate fingers would knit, or
knot, or embroider, the garter, the purfe,
or the waiftcoat; all of which were deftined pledges of affection for her Walftein. Ever defirous of finding new fources
to give him pleafure, every action had
that for its object. For him only did fhe
exift, and continually would fhe invent
pretexts either to go into his apartment, or
invite him into hers. Though fhe faw no
perfon but him and the High Chamberlain, who fupped with them almoft every

evening,

evening, never was she dull for want of company. Far from that, she continually refufed the folicitations of the Baron to prefent her at court, feemed moft defirous of prolonging her retreat, and, with mild and timid eyes turned to Walftein, faid, "never before had she been fo happy!" Yet, notwithftanding all the thoufand hourly repeated proofs of love which Caroline no longer fought to hide, ftill did the Count, fafcinated by fear, and dreading to yield to the fenfations by which he was continually affaulted, repel truth, and retain foregone and chimerical conclufions.

"Not for me," would he fay, "is it to be beloved. No, the affectionate, the tender, the adorable Caroline has the art of giving to friendfhip—alas! what did I fay?

I say? Not even to friendfhip, but, to fimple gratitude, all the appearance and expreffion of love... It is not the prefence of Walftein, but the remembrance of Lindorf, by which fhe thus is animated; and to him, doubtlefs, doth fhe fecretly addrefs all thofe affecting attentions, thofe tender fpeeches, and thofe fweet looks, which may not have me for their true object—What! know I not that fhe loves Lindorf! Nay, that him fhe ought to love!—Yet, fhould it be true!—Should it be me!—Should my prefent intents, which diftract and rend my heart, make me the moft ungrateful of men! Should that blifs of angels, which I am referving for another, be deftined by Caroline for me!—Alas, it cannot be.—Oh! Caroline! Caroline!—Yet, how may I know

what

what paſſes in her heart, without acquainting her with the ſecrets of my own; without diſcovering the paſſion by which I am conſumed? And yet how may I make this known, certain, as I am, that duty, generoſity, and compaſſion would dictate her anſwer? Though ſhe love me not, her preſent actions and manner prove ſhe would not an inſtant heſitate to ſacrifice her heart and her happineſs to me."

Thus tormented, thus agitated, by hope and fear, did the Count make both himſelf and the tender Caroline miſerable. But ſenſations ſo violent cannot long endure: Lindorf comes not, nor will the Count find, either in delicacy or friendſhip, the power to reſiſt love that thus is induſtrious to convince him it is mutual.

One

One evening, when the High Chamberlain was detained at court, the Count supped alone with Caroline, who was more tender, more endearing, more enchanting than ufual. If fhe *faid* not I love, it was almoft impoffible to mifunderftand her *actions.* The emotion, the agitation of Walftein augmented every moment, and he muft either betray his feelings or fly the danger. He juft had ftrength fufficient to perform this painful tafk, but it was the laft effort of reafon. Shut up in his own apartment, he reflected on his prefent ftate, his love, his claims, and the conduct of Caroline.

"No," faid he, "it is not, it cannot be, illufive. I am beloved. I no longer have caufe to doubt. If I touch her hand I feel it tremulous; or if fhe takes mine fhe gently

ly

ly holds and preffes it, unwilling it fhould
be withdrawn; if I quit her with mourn-
ful looks her eyes follow me; and, this very
evening, I beheld them moiftened with her
tears. All the animation, all the tendernefs of affection, were painted in her countenance; and yet I left her; yet I forbore
to kneel at her feet; yet I forbear to tell
her how infinitely I adore her; neglect
to fupplicate a confirmation of my happinefs, and of that love which every incident
tends but to confirm."

Never had the idea prefented itfelf to
him with fo much force and certainty: it
enrapt him fo far that, no longer liftening
to ought but fweet hope, he determined
to return, confefs his paffion, and obtain
from Caroline an avowal of hers, of which
he no longer doubted. All his oaths, re-
folutions,

folutions, and projects difappeared; all were annihilate; he forgot that Lindorf had exiftence: Caroline, only, he beheld! His Caroline! To him united, by him beloved, and him loving; nor was there longer mortal man who fhould bear away this treafure of his foul!—In an inftant, Walftein, again, is in her apartment. He fees her not, but he hears her guittar, hears the melody of founds that vibrate to his heart; he approaches, foftly, a door, half open, that leads to a fmall chamber, whither Caroline has retired. It was her favourite apartment; there fhe paffed an hour, every evening, before fhe went to bed, reading, finging, or playing. Caroline was half undreffed, reclining in an arm chair, and gently touching her guittar as fhe fang. The air was melancholy, and fhe feemed deeply affected;

affected; ftopped occafionally, and put her
handkerchief up to her eyes; then again continued, with lefs power, but more paffion,
in her voice. Walftein thought he had
known all her favourite fongs, yet this was
new to him. He liftened with mute attention, earneft to hear the words. Caroline
fang fo low that he could only catch now
and then a line, one of which, however,
ftruck him, and he liftened ftill more eagerly. At laft he diftinctly heard the following part of a ftanza:

   Ah! wherefore, Love, or whither fly,
   In fearch of blifs I'd fain impart ?
   If thou forfak'ft me, how may I
   Hope cherifh in this bleeding heart ?

The expreffion, the marked tendernefs,
with which fhe fang, were fufficient proofs
Caroline's complaint had reference to a
real,

real, not an imaginary lover. But who
was this lover? Was it Lindorf? Was it
Walftein? Diffidence and doubt again poffeffed his heart; he looks, he liftens, and
prefently the fhadowy pleafure of doubt
itfelf vanifhes. Caroline laid her guittar
in her lap, and untied a black ribband
which fhe always wore around her neck.
Till then the Count had fuppofed it was
only an ornament, but he faw with furprife
a miniature picture was pendant to it, and
which Caroline had always carried concealed
in her bofom. Too far off to diftinguifh the
features, he yet could fee, as fhe put it to
the candle, that it was the uniform of an
officer in the Pruffian guards; it was, therefore, the uniform and the portrait of Lindorf! Caroline, at firft, fixed her eyes upon
it, then preffed it to her heart, and next

to

to her lips, with extreme paffion. The tears ran down her cheeks, and fell upon the picture; fhe carefully wiped them off, again looked and fighed, laid it on the table, took up her guitar and fang another ftanza of the fame fong, which the Count diftinctly heard.

> The fole, the fov'reign, balm I find,
> Dear emblem of my Love, is thee;
> Thou bear'ft his features, but his mind,
> Ah! who fhall paint its energy?
> Then wherefore, Love, or whither fly,
> In fearch of blifs I'd fain impart?
> If thou forfak'ft me, how may I
> Hope cherifh in this bleeding heart?

When fhe had ended, fhe once more took up her picture, gave it another kifs, tied it round her neck again, and, as fhe put it down her bofom, faid, with a mix-

ture of tenderneſs and chagrin, "thou, however, ſhalt never forſake me;" then, taking
up her candle, paſſed into her bedchamber,
after having rung for her attendants, without ſo much as looking towards the half
open door. The action of riſing, the removal of Caroline, and the darkneſs, in
which Walſtein was left, awakened him
from a kind of ſtupor into which he had
ſunk; from a dream of terror, which, as
he awoke, inſtead of vaniſhing, was confirmed! All his imagined happineſs was fled,
and again he was ingulphed in wretched-
neſs at the very inſtant imagination had
conducted him to the ultimate of bliſs!
Yet, ever generous, even in the horrors of
deſpair, his firſt intention was, when he
had ſomewhat recovered himſelf, to go
immediately to Caroline, not to intercede
for himſelf, but to aſſure her Lindorf,

her

her fugitive, her beloved, fhould return, fhould be hers. The arrival of the maids, however, prevented him from executing this his defign, and he prefently afterwards felt he no longer had the fortitude, per-fonally, to tell her he would for ever yield her to another. His heart palpitated with fuch violence that fuch a declaration feem-ed as if it muft have coft him his life, and he even fhuddered left, had he feen her at that moment, inftead of acting as friend-fhip and juftice required, he, in his de-lirium, fhould have fuffered paffion to in-vade the rights of love.

No, he would fee her no more! He might not, could not, durft not, fee her more! He ftill found fufficient virtue to fly, to reftore her to liberty, but never to bid.

her

her an eternal adieu; or again to gaze on those impaffioned eyes, the danger of which he had fo recently proved. He returned therefore to his chamber, where he paffed fome hours in a ftate of undefcribable anguifh, incapable of determination; of all certitude whether Love or Generofity, Lindorf or Walftein, fhould prevail. He wrote letter after letter to Caroline: in one he claimed his rights, and endeavoured to move her compaffion; detefting his tyranny, and tearing this, he began another, in which he bad her for ever farewell, without the leaft mention of his own excruciating pangs. "What," faid he, again, with increafing agitation, tearing the paper, "fhall fhe even remain ignorant of the adoration in which I hold her? Shall I die without fo much as exciting her compaffion?"

fion?" He began once more; once more
painted his love in all its enthufiafm, and
the facrifice he was about to make in all
its horrors. Still lefs fatisfied than ever,
he tried anew to write with more mode-
ration; and again and again he tried, and
was each time alike unfuccefsful.

At length, however, the fatigued and
exhaufted fpirit fank into a gloomy calm,
and Walftein came to a firm and irre-
vocable determination.—This was to go
betimes in the morning to the King, who
never was in bed long after day-break, and
to whom he was never denied admittance,
to obtain, immediately, without further
let or delay, a divorce; to fend it inftantly
to Caroline, and as inftantly to leave Potfdam, retire to his eftate at Walftein, and

there

there make proper preparations for travels which he knew not when he should end. The more he reflected on prefent circumftances, and the contrary paffions by which he fuppofed himfelf and Caroline tormented, the more did he perfift in this project, and deeply regretted not having put it in execution immediately after his arrival at Berlin; inftead of fuffering himfelf to be thus feduced by the fafcinating pleafure of living with Caroline. "Long fince," faid he, "would fhe then have been eafy, and I myfelf perhaps lefs wretched; I then fhould not have known the enchantment of her fmiles, the irrefiftible allurement of her friendfhip, and the bewitching influence of her attentions: or, at leaft, I fhould have known them but in part; attentions which I interpreted into love, and which

which might have fupplied its abfence, had I remained ignorant that fhe loves another, over whofe memory fhe in fecret mourns. —Mourn! Does Caroline mourn? Caroline! For whom I would facrifice a thoufand lives! And fhall I hefitate then to yield up my happinefs?"

The thought was moft natural and appeafing to the noble heart of Walftein. He wrote, or rather began to write a letter to fend Caroline when he fhould have obtained a divorce. He afterwards wrote alfo to the High Chamberlain, to give this tranfaction fuch a colouring as that he might not impute it to his daughter, or Lindorf. Thefe letters he put in his pocket, and, aided by his valet de chambre, made every neceffary preparation for

his

his travels. As he fuppofed he was no
more to vifit Berlin, he paffed the reft of
the night in putting his papers in order,
and collecting certain of them, which he
meant to take with him. As foon as day
appeared, he fet off for Potfdam, where
the King then was, and entreated a fecret
audience.

How, in the mean time, was poor Caroline employed?—She awoke from a
fweet fleep, which had calmed her inquietude, and already began to be impatient
again to fee that dear and cruel hufband
who thus fled her embraces, and whom fhe
yet had hoped to win by affection and
perfeverance. Nay, indeed, fhe had lately
flattered herfelf with fuccefs, and that
there was very little of the extraordinary

in

in his conduct.   He feemed pleafed to be
with her, feldom left her during the day,
and had all thofe little preventive cares
which are fo peculiar to love; fhe often
caught him looking paffionately at her,
and, once, furprifed him ardently kiffing a
ringlet of her hair.   What more was neceffary to Caroline? Educated in the utmoft innocence, without friendfhip or other
converfation than that of the chafte Canonefs, never having read other books than
what fhe recommended, fhe was moft happy when in the fight and hearing of her
hufband.—To fuppofe herfelf beloved, to
pafs her life in his company, was blifs fu-
preme; and when he quitted her, at night,
her only chagrin was that of being fepa-
rated from him till the morrow, Thefe,
likewife, were the only moments in which

she longer doubted of his love; ", for," said she, ", he might stay, if he pleased; we still could converse a little longer; or read, or sing, and then, when I awoke in the morning, I should have the dear pleasure of seeing him immediately. For why might he not as well sleep in my chamber as in his own? Oh! that I durst but tell him so!— But he does not love so much to be with me as I do to be with him; he pines not as I do when we are asunder."

Then would Caroline weep without knowing why; then would she gaze on her little picture, kiss it, repeat those tender things she durst not say to the original, commit it again to her bosom, go to sleep with it, and, on the morrow, when she met

the

the Count, no more remember any thing
but the pleafure of being in his prefence.

This was nearly her diurnal hiftory;
though, on the evening we have been defcribing, fhe was more than ufually moved
by the emotion of the Count; and, particularly, by his fudden retreat, which came
fo unexpected, and which, by the manner
of it, had produced this effect. She, then,
began to reflect there was fomething extremely fingular in the conduct of her hufband; fuch frequent inequality of behaviour, fo many contradictions, and circumftances fhe knew not how to explain, raifed
her attention. Was fhe beloved, or was
fhe not? To anfwer this queftion fhe endeavoured to recollect every incident that
had any relation to Walftein from the

D 6 moment

moment after their arrival at Ronebourg. While thus ruminating, a fong fhe had compofed, at the time the Count endeavoured to avoid her, and when fhe imagined herfelf hated by him, was recollected, and the recollection affected her; fhe fang it, and her tendernefs was redoubled. Then it was that the Count had overheard her, unfortunately, as fhe was ending the fong, which was as follows.

When now no longer ftarting fears,
With boding ills, difturb my peace;
Now love and duty dry my tears,
And bid my former terrors ceafe;
Ah! where, my Love, or whither fly,
In fearch of blifs I'd fain impart?
If thou forfak'ft me, how may I
Hope cherifh in this bleeding heart?

Thy

Thy daily forrow, nightly care,
Each word, each look, to love I gave ;
Love drove away the fiend defpair,
And flew to fnatch me from the grave.
Then wherefore, now, or whither fly,
In fearch of blifs I'd fain impart ?
If love forfakes me, how may I
Hope cherifh in this bleeding heart ?

But if, deceiv'd, not love had aught
In what fo well with love agrees,
To life, ah ! wherefore am I brought,
To perifh by a worfe difeafe ?
Ah ! wherefore, Love, or whither fly,
In fearch of blifs I'd fain impart ?
If thou forfak'ft me, how may I
Hope cherifh in this bleeding heart ?

The fole, the fov'reign balm I find,
Dear emblem of my Love, is thee ;
Thou bear'ft his features, but his mind,
Ah ! who fhall paint its energy ?

Then

Then wherefore, Love, or whither fly,

In fearch of blifs I'd fain impart?

If thou forfak'ſt me, how may I

Hope cherifh in this bleeding heart?

Had the Count heard the firſt ſtanzas he muſt have known they related to him; but the latter, and, efpecially, the addrefs to the picture, wholly led him into error. His portrait it could not be; and the energy was the energy of Lindorf, who, flying, thus ſacrificed his happinefs to his friend.

As to Caroline, having fung, wept, and kiffed her picture, ſhe went to bed much relieved and more tranquil. " He loves me," thought ſhe; " I am fure he loves me; but he believes he is not beloved. He remembers the repugnance which I ſo unjuſtly, ſo unkindly, ſhewed on the day of our marriage. And can he fuppofe I ſtill am

unjuſt

unjuſt and unkind? But I will undeceive him, will forget my fears, will commit all the ſecrets of my heart to the boſom of my huſband, and prove how totally this fro-ward heart is changed. To-morrow, yes, to-morrow 1 am determined I will tell him all; tell him every day, and every moment that I adore him, and we then ſhall ſee whether he will fly from me thus each evening after ſupper."

This reſolution made her perfectly calm; ſhe ſlept in peace, had delightful dreams, awaked with the pureſt ſenſations of plea-ſure, and was more than ever determined to execute the project ſhe had conceived on the over night. No more ſhe felt the ſame fears, the ſame diffidence of herſelf. Walſtein loves her; ſhe is convinced he loves her. Doubts and recollections of the

paſt

paft are the occafion of his continued referve.   Unable any longer to. fupport
thefe, fhe, with a word, will expel them
all.   Yes, fhe will prove to him, by
a thoufand incidents, that he is the fole
object of her affection; that he lives and
reigns fingly and wholly in her heart.
Poor Caroline! That heart of thine, fo
innocent, fo tender, may not contain its
tranfports, while, in this delirium of blifs,
thou rememberest it fhall no longer have
a thought concealed from thy beloved
Walftein ; from that noble hufband to
whom thou art indebted for thy life, and
to whofe happinefs this life thou meaneft
to confecrate.   But, ah! that heart not
yet knows half it has to fuffer !

Timidity is natural to youth, and efpecially to youth educated as Caroline had
been.

been. The superior virtues and wisdom
of Walltein commanded a respect which
not even the most mild benevolence could
wholly obliterate. It was therefore that
Caroline had been silent so long; and even
now, determined as she is, she knows not
what means are best, how to behave, or
what to say; and the more the moment
approaches, the more her embarrassment
is increased. Oh! how does she regret her
dear Mamma, who, had she lived, would,
long since, have been her faithful inter-
preter; the voluntary pledge of her truth
and tenderness! But how might she herself explain them? Should she write?——
She began, but her emotion was too great,
her hand trembled, she could find no ex-
pressions that could convey her feelings;
no words were adequate to her ideas;
she could not frame a single phrase——

"No,"

"No," faid fhe, "it will be better to go, to run to him, to throw myfelf into his arms, to fay—Perhaps I may not fay a word, but furely he will underftand my filence; furely he will not be able to look at me without imagining what I wifh to fay; he will pardon me, will difpel my fears; referve, diffidence, and doubt, fhall vanifh all; he fhall be wholly mine, and I wholly his; the happieft of wives and of women!"

The thought inflames her ardour, fhe kiffes her little portrait to increafe her courage, and flies to the apartment of the moft beloved of hufbands! She enters— But no hufband is there! He feems not even there to have flept!—A large trunk, in the midft of the chamber, round which are various other packets, feems to announce a removal, a removal, or a journey.—Caroline shakes from head to foot! Scarcely has she strength to ring the bell!—A footman appears; tremblingly she asks—" Where is my Lord the Count ?"

The footman, surprised at the question, answers, " I thought my Lady had known"—

" Known, what ?"

" That my Lord set off betimes this morning."

" Set off!——God !"——

" William, his valet de chambre, has been up all night, making ready. He has left orders that this trunk and these packets should follow. He does not know where

where my Lord is going, but he believes
to England."

" England!——Leave me!"

The footman goes, and Caroline finks
in the firft chair fhe can ftagger to; where,
for the fecond time in her life, fhe feels
all the affliction, all the torture of defpair-
ing love. A fecond time fees the man fhe
loves neglect, abandon, fly from her!—
But what a difference between the prefent
and the former flight! When, at Rindaw, Lindorf left her, it was neceffity, it
was virtue, it was her own wifh; the feparation was a cruel one, but the reflection
that fhe had done her duty was, indeed,
the moft effective confolation! Befide, fhe
knew fhe was beloved, and that he who
fled partook of all her affliction. Far
different

different are her prefent pangs, which every circumftance but augments.   Not a clandeftine lover but a beloved hufband flies, in whom every hope of future felicity cen-ters.   A hufband that hates her; or could he abandon her in a manner like this?—At what a moment too!

"Oh God! Then when I flew to him with open arms, when I imagined how un-fpeakable his joy would be; then to de-part, without mentioning the leaft word of his intent, without feeing me once again! This muft be hatred, or a moft cruel, moft unconquerable indifference! Yet, yefterday evening, how did he look at me! With what tendernefs did he take my hand, and prefs it to his heart!—It is true, he repulfed it again with terror, and inftantly left me!—For ever left me!—No, no;

no; it cannot, it fhall not be. He is no
diffembler: Walftein is not the moft bar-
barous of all human beings.—It is error—
The 'fervant is miftaken; he will return;
yes, he will, he muft; and here will I
wait his return.

Scarcely had the poor diftreffed Caroline
indulged this momentary glimpfe of hope,
which fomewhat recovered her funk fpi-
rits, before the footman re-entered, and
brought her a packet of papers, fealed up.
—"It comes from my Lord, the Count;
the courier is this moment arrived from
Potfdam."

Caroline had juft fufficient ftrength to
receive it, and, by a fign, bid him retire.
And now behold her alone, holding the
packet fhe dares not open. Life or death
lies

lies there fealed up. It was large, and addreffed *to the Countefs Caroline, Baronefs of Lichtfield, in her Hotel*—It was ftrange, this; moft ftrange!—" What! will he not call me by his name? God of Heaven! Is it poffible?" Her trembling fingers break the feals; and, as the cover is torn, fhe finds, firft, a parchment deed, next, three letters, and, laft, an unfealed open paper, on which her eyes are rivetted.

Souls of fympathy, that now with Caroline remain in fearful fufpenfe, imagine a paper, a fatal paper, figned by the king, fealed by the king; imagine a deed, or rather a declaration of 'divorce, by which *the King confents to the diffolution of the marriage of Edmund Auguftus Walftein and. Caroline of Lichtfield, decrees it null and void,*

void, and the parties free to contract else-
where!

Yes, the eyes of Caroline were rivetted, wild, yet shed not a single tear! Thus, a while, she stood: at length, the writings dropped from her hands, a dark cloud enveloped her, a cold sweat overspread her pale face; she sees no more, breathes no more, a universal palpitation seizes her; her last thought is a hope that the hand of death is upon her, and she sinks into insensibility!

Thus did she some time remain; and, when nature began somewhat to revive, she imagined she had been in a fearful dream; but not long did this deception continue; the chamber, the trunks, the letters, the paper were there, witnesses of the reality

of

of her wretchednefs.   She looks at the direction of thofe letters.   The firft is to
her father, the fecond to Caroline, and is
rejected with horror.—" What can he fay,
while thus he murders me, while thus he
himfelf diffolves our union?"

She examines the third and what is her
furprife! It is directed to the Baron of
Lindorf, at Walftein-houfe, Berlin; and
at the bottom of the direction is written,
*I conjure Caroline to give this letter, with her .
own hand, to my friend, the very moment he
arrives, which muft be foon*—" To Lindorf!"
exclaimed fhe.   " At his own houfe!
And to me the letter entrufted! Oh God!
Oh God! what can be the meaning of
this! Lindorf here!—Could he be capable!—Is he the caufe of?—Oh! would
to God it may be jealoufy! How eafily
fhall I be able to prove it groundlefs!"

Caroline eagerly takes up the rejected letter, addreſſed to her, opens it, begins to read, and hope revives in her heart. —No! not jealouſy, not hatred, not indifference, not reſentment, are there; but generoſity, delicacy, love; paſſionate love, tender, exceſſive, heroic love; and in an inſtant Caroline paſſes from the depths of miſery to the pureſt heaven of bliſs. " He loves me! He loves me!" ſaid ſhe. " He loves me, and our marriage is not diſſolved! Soon ſhall he know Caroline loves him alſo; will be his, and his only; will exiſt for him, with him, by him, and never, while life endures, will leave him more!" Bleſſed as this letter was, ſcarcely could ſhe end it, ſo eager was ſhe to give orders, inſtantly, to prepare the poſt cha- riot; but, while it is preparing, again ſhe reads, again ſhe devours its contents. The

words

words are hofts of angels, and the fmall paper the infinite regions of blifs. |

" Dear and tender Caroline, ceafe to
" grieve, ceafe to fubdue your feelings;
" not to a tyrant has the care of your
" happinefs been committed. The tears
" I have fo lately feen fall, on the picture
" of a regretted lover, fhall be the laft
" which for this reafon you fhall fhed——
" Oh! may my prayers be heard, and
" may the God of goodnefs grant, as an
" ample reward for my own fufferings,
" that her whom I adore may be hence-
" forth, and for ever, happy; then fhall I,
" though feparate and far, far from her,
" though knowing her another's, ftill be
" able to fupport exiftence. Yes, angel
" of my foul, be happy; be his whom
" your heart hath felected, and who merits,

E 2   " at

" at leaſt as much as mortal may, a bleſ-
" ſing ſo ſupreme. .No longer ſhall your
" ſenſibility, by virtue tortured, lament
" a union which your ſoul abhors; no
" longer ſhall you ſhed thoſe ſecret and
" corroding tears, which I would rather
" periſh than be the cauſe of. Love and
" duty ſhall be allied.

" Oh Caroline! ſtill do I hear thoſe
" moving, thoſe paſſionate ſounds, dic-
" tated by grief, and addreſſed to the ob-
" ject of your tenderneſs. But complain
" no more; no more reproach him with
" an involuntary abſence which he to
" friendſhip thought he owed. He ſhall
" be reſtored to your arms, Caroline; you
" ſhall ſee him, kneeling at your feet, and
" preſently ſhall you both forget your
" former pains.

                                    " Pardon,

"Pardon, Oh! pardon, Caroline, that
" I so long have neglected to give you
" happiness and joy. From the moment
" that first I learned your secret, that fatal
" moment when I saw you expiring, when
" I felt there was a degree of misery su-
" perior even to that of resigning you, I
" then swore to unite you to each other.
" Caroline, thou thyself canst witness how
" sacred I have held the wife of my friend,
" the beloved of Lindorf—yet will I own,
" blinded by my passion, I have had mo-
" mentary illusions, have thought it possi-
" ble I might myself be ineffably blessed,
" have misinterpreted the efforts of duty
" and virtue into softer sensations, and had
" almost prepared the iron scourge of
" never-ending regret for myself, and
" pining grief and melancholy for
" thee. But it is past, the charm is

E 3 "broken,

" broken, and I feel it is time to fly. Yes,
" in a delirium of hope was I almoſt loſt;
" but, with the firſt rays of returning day,
" I will depart to obtain what ſhall for
" ever baniſh all ſuch future raſh hopes,
" to which I have too, too, weakly yielded.
" I go to reſtore you to yourſelf; or, rather,
" to the original of that picture you hold
" ſo dear. Farewell, Caroline; I perceive
" I ſay what I ought not; I ſhall give a
" pang to your generous and tender heart,
" by expoſing the weakneſs of my own.
" At length, however, dear Caroline;
" know me for what I am. Know that;
" be my miſery what it may in quitting
" you, in renouncing you thus eternally,
" it ſtill would be infinitely greater were
" I to remain and uſurp thoſe rights which
" are due to love alone. To poſſeſs the
" perſon of Caroline, and to know that
                              " another

" another poffeffes her heart, to be equally
" an impediment to her happinefs and the
" happinefs of a dear and refpected friend,
" this were impoffible to fupport! But to
" be a fpectator of, or, at leaft, to imagine,
" your mutual felicity, will fpread a gleam
" of comfort over defponding life. Ca-
" roline will owe that felicity to me, will-
" think of me with tendernefs and grati-
" tude, and thus, while I live, I fhall live
" certain of her friendfhip, and when I die
" fhe will fhed a tear over my tomb.———
" Farewell!—Caroline, farewell! I fly to
" merit the friendfhip I fo earneftly covet.

" *Berlin, five o'clock in the morning.*

" *P. S.   Dated at Potfdam, ten o'clock,*
" *and after having had an audience with the.*
" *King.*

" All is over, the chains which have
" ever hung fo heavy on Caroline are

" broken.

"broken. She is free, and shall soon be
"Lindorf's. Oh! tell me, tell me, Ca-
" roline, that you are happy. Let me have
" this confolation——My friend is igno-
" rant of the blifs that awaits him. I know
" his generous friendfhip, and the fame
" feelings that drove him from Rindaw,
" and his country, may, perhaps, ftill make
" him refufe this felicity. This muft not
" be: to prevent it I have written a
" letter, addreffed to him, which will end
" all his fcruples, and prove that he only
" can contribute to the fmall degree of
" happinefs of which Walftein is now ca-
" pable, by making himfelf and Caroline
" happy.

" I ftill have a favour to afk, and, furely,
" Caroline, in a moment like this, will not,
" by refufal, increafe my griefs. No, I
" know

" know her heart too well.—It is to accept
" the houſe ſhe at preſent inhabits. You
" like its ſituation, Caroline; your apart-
" ments pleaſe you; they were deſigned
" for you, furniſhed for you, and never
" ſhall any one but you inhabit them—
" You will not, ſurely you will not, by a
" cruel denial, make your wretched friend
" ſtill more wretched.

" Again and again, farewell! Dear and
" adored Caroline, farewell!—And is it
" true, then, that you are no longer mine,
" that I no longer have the leaſt right?—
" What talk I of rights, I never had any;
" thoſe the heart only can accord, and, at
" preſent, I ſhall be certain of your pity
" and eſteem. Ah would you but ſome-
" times write to me, would you but de-
" ſcribe your happineſs—But no, it can-

" not

" not be : never muſt I write to the wife of
" Lindorf. If Caroline of Lichtfield will
" for once deign to anſwer me, only once,
" before ſhe bears another name, her letter
" will reach me at Walſtein, where I ſhall
" remain eight days, before I ſet off 'to
" Dreſden, to viſit my ſiſter.

" I am going to depart !—And ſhall I
" never ſee you more ? Shall thoſe hea-
" venly hours which, by your ſide, I have
" paſſed, never return ? Shall I never more
" liſten to your ſweet voice ?—Caroline, I
" rave, for never, while thought remains,
" will you be abſent from my imagination.
" Whatever hoſpitable, or inhoſpitable,
" land may contain my body, my ſoul will
" be ever preſent with you.

" Herewith

" Herewith I fend the King's confirma-
" tion of your liberty, a letter to your
" father, one to—to your hufband, and
" the deed of conveyance of Walftein-houfe.
" Let me know, at leaft, that you have re-
" ceived thofe papers; let me, once again,
" entreat you to tell me you are happy,
" and all the purpofes of this world are
" ended with

    " EDMUND AUGUSTUS WALSTEIN."

Again this dear letter is read till the
chariot is ready, except juft for a moment
that Caroline runs into her own apartment
to fetch the manufcript of Lindorf; the
picture, that principal caufe of miftake, is
warm in her bofom. And now fhe de-
parts, entreating, conjuring the poftillions
to be expeditious, and, notwithftanding
all their endeavours to oblige fo fweet a

        E 6   petitioner,

petitioner, ftill fhe finds they go but flowly. The Count was fome hours before her, and yet, fo great was the diligence fhe ufed, he had not been very long at Walftein before fhe arrived. Shut up in his clofet, a prey to the moft violent grief, infenfible of every thing but the lofs of Caroline, whom he never was more to behold, dead even to the confolations of virtue, he there had retired from the world, and the fight of human being. A momentary gleam of comfort had come over him when he firft was met by his vaffals and fervants. Louifa, Juftin, and the aged Joffelin, had been at the head of them, had fallen and cla'ped the knees of their benefactor, had prefented their two little boys, and, with bleffings and prayers, and fmiles, and tears, had given him falutation. Louifa was pregnant again. " Oh ! my Lord," faid

fhe,

ſhe, "your arrival is the forerunner of happineſs. I ſhall have a little girl, for which
ſo often I have prayed; and now my Lord
is married, if my Lady, the Counteſs, will
but have the goodneſs to ſtand Godmother,
and let my child be chriſtened after her, I
ſhall never be thankful enough for the
favor."

The grateful Louiſa ſpoke daggers! The
Count could not ſupport it.—"Alas! child,
I am—I am no longer"—Walſtein was
obliged to break off abruptly and fly to
conceal the burſting efforts of nature.

Theſe good people ſtill were aſſembled in
the court, and with them ſome of the villagers, who all were lamenting the grief in
which they had ſeen their good lord, when
Caroline arrived. She opened the door,
ſprang

fprang from her chariot, and, without feeing or hearing perfon or object that fur-
rounded her, exclaimed, "Where is he?
Where is the Count?"

William flew!—"Here is my Lady the
Countefs!"—

" Yes, dear William, here am I! Where
is he? Lead me to him inftantly!"

William ran before her, pointed to his
mafter's clofet door, and retired. Caroline opens it, runs, falls into his arms,
and in a broken voice exclaims, "My Lord!
My Hufband!—Wherefore haft thou
quitted thus thy Caroline, who adores thee,
who loves thee and thee only in all the
world, and whom thou wilt kill fhouldeft
thou abandon her?"

The

The hafte with which she ran, her eagernefs, her fobs, all cut speech short and interrupted refpiration; her head reclined on
the shoulder of the Count, her arms hung
round his neck, and her tears fell into his
bofom. Wallftein was not lefs agitated
than herfelf; at laft, taking her in his arms
and placing her on a fopha, he falls at her
feet.

" Caroline!——Caroline!——Is it you,
Caroline?——Is it, or is it fome pitying
angel who has affumed your form? Can
what I have heard be poffible?"

"Doubt it not, doubt it not! Here, here
(Caroline untied the ribband and took the
portrait from her bofom) look, behold
the picture I love; nay, look at it well;
fay whofe likenefs it is; behold who thus

entirely

entirely poffeffes my heart, and for whom alone I would live and die !"

Walftein looked!—With aftonifhment looked!—It was he!—Good God! he himfelf! At leaft fuch as he himfelf had been; and Caroline proved fhe ftill beheld him as he had been, and that, to her, he had undergone no change. True it was, indeed, that he every day became more like his portrait, and that, at prefent, the likenefs even could not be miftaken. But by what magic, what miracle could this portrait, of the exiftence of which the Count himfelf was ignorant, fall into the hands of Caroline, be worn next her heart, and become the object of her deareft, her tendereft careffes? He looks, he faulters, he is ready to fink under the excefs, and yet cannot he believe it real! It is a heavenly

dream

dream out of which he fears to awake!
Few are his words, but thofe few all are ex-
preſſive of rapture, aſtoniſhment, and remaining doubt. As ſoon as paſſion would
permit, Caroline, bluſhing, drew from her
pocket all the letters and the manuſcript
which Lindorf had left her—" Take thefe,"
faid ſhe, " read, and you will know all. No
more will I have any ſecrets for my Walſtein; they have already made me too
wretched.—Yes, I loved Lindorf; at leaſt,
I had fenſations that bore ſome reſem-
blance to thofe I feel at preſent. What the
difference is you yourſelf ſhall judge. When
Lindorf left me, at Rindaw, I wept; yes,
wept, and not a little; but my grief ſoon found
alleviation, ſoon ſubſided, and ſoon did
this ſmall picture become dearer to my
heart than Lindorf. This morning, on the
contrary, I wept not, when I received the
fearful

fearful fentence of feparation. Not a tear
efcaped: but I thought either death
or diftraction muft have been the inftantaneous effect, and fhould you perfift
in that your dreadful defign it would be
as though you were to fay to me *Caroline*, *I
wifh thee dead*—But, Oh! rather fay 'Caroline, I wifh thee mine, and mine thou ever
fhalt be'—Here—here is the paper! The—
the Divorce! Look how infignificant it is
at prefent!"

It was torn in a thoufand pieces, and
Caroline caft it with indignation into the
fire—Walftein could not utter a word! He
gazed, he wept, he took her hand, preffed it to his lips, to his heart—He gazed
again, and exclamations, without connec-
tion, without meaning, fucceeded each other.
He took up his own picture, and, in his delirium,

lirium, kiffed it with tranfport! It was the facred proof of the affection of his dear Caroline !

Caroline preffed him, once more, to read the manufcript, but this he could not, this would have been to have taken his eyes off her, and have robbed himfelf of moments the moft precious, the moft ecftatic the human heart knows.—" No, dear Caroline, do not, do not afk me to read now. I do read, I read your heart, I there find I am beloved; and what farther knowledge can I want?"

" But you know not the hiftory of the portrait." " No matter; I know it dear to you, and that is all I wifh to know."

" Nay, but hear, at leaft, that it was
Lindorf

Lindorf who taught me to eſtimate the worth of Walſtein; who firſt inſpired admiration, which was afterward productive of love."

" Lindorf!"

"Yes, let me do him juſtice; to Lindorf you are indebted for the heart of your Caroline."

" To Lindorf!——Generous Friend!"

" To you he owes every thing."

" No, no, I am indebted to him for more than life."

Walſtein then took the manuſcript and read, and Caroline preſently ſaw the ſtruggling efforts of ſenſibility; often was he obliged to ſtop, and endeavoured to ſtifle his

tears,

tears, and as often did he tell Caroline, with a broken and paſſionate voice, that Lindorf moſt merited her affection. Caroline, with her angel hand, ſtopped his mouth, and obliged him to continue his reading. He paſſed rapidly over events which were already familiar to his memory, but when he came to the epocha of the firſt meeting of Lindorf and Caroline, his very foul ſeemed a part of the paper, each ſyllable, each phraſe was devoured, and he read with his eyes only, for circumſtances like theſe might not be read aloud. Caroline, with fixed looks, continually endeavoured to diſcover the different ſenſations by which he was agitated.

When he had ended, he gave her back the manuſcript in a manner that ſhewed how much he had been moved.—"I ſee," ſaid

said he, " I have a wife and a friend such as never man had, and that they both have sacrificed their own felicity to mine—Ah! wherefore, Caroline, did you oblige me to read this manuscript? Why not leave me in that blessed dream into which I so lately had been lulled?"

" A dream! Unkind Walstein! Is that an epithet for feelings such as mine? Do you forget that this is your picture?"— The word picture, pronounced with the utmost affection, was convincing, and restored the Count all his confidence and bliss. —"And now" said she, "that you have read your own story, and that of Lindorf, listen to the history of my heart."

Caroline, then, circumstantially, related all that had passed from the moment of
their

their marriage : the innocence with which
she suppofed fhe loved Lindorf as a brother
and her terror at firft imagining him a lover;
the fcene of the garden, of the pavilion,
her grief, her tears, her regret, her ftruggles, all were told. She next informed him
how, induced by efteem and admiration at
reading his letters to Lindorf, fhe had begun to think of him, to look at and love
his portrait ; fpoke of what fhe felt on receiving the letter in which he propofed to
leave his country, and of the delicacy, the
fenfations, and the mixture of chagrin that
had occafioned her anfwer. When fhe
came to the court yard of Ronebourg, " I
proteft, I vow," faid fhe, " it was agitation
only at finding myfelf fo unexpectedly in
the prefence of a hufband whom I had fo
cruelly wronged, and by whom I had fo
much caufe to be hated; it was not Lindorf.

dorf. No, you long had utterly effaced every impreſſion he had made upon my heart."

The Count liſtened in rapture. He was enchanted, and took care not to give her the leaſt interruption. With what en-thuſiaſm, what truth, what eloquence, what affection, did ſhe ſpeak! How did ſhe dwell on every circumſtance of her re-covery at Ronebourg, of her hopes and fears ſince their arrival at Berlin, and her continual intention of explaining her feel-ings; of the timidity by which ſhe was re-ſtrained; of her deſire to pleaſe him, to win his affection, to attach him wholly to herſelf, and make him happy; of her grief at her ill ſucceſs, her reſolution, that very morning, of ſpeaking, and her extreme af-fliction at finding him gone; of her de-ſpair at receiving the fatal packet, and

of

of the joy that fucceeded when fhe was fo
fully convinced, from his letter, how dearly
fhe was beloved by her hufband. All was
expreffed with that rapidity, that perfuafion,
that paffion, which fo entirely remove doubt.
—" At prefent," added fhe, " you are as
perfectly acquainted with Caroline as fhe is
with herfelf; I have nothing more to relate, except to paint how happy I am. Oh!
but how? It is wholly impoffible! I love,
am beloved, and may, without a blufh, receive and return all the moft endearing
proofs of love! Yes, my dear Lord, our
hearts are now acquainted with each other.
Eftimate mine by your own!"

Walftein would have replied, would have
entered into explanations concerning his
own conduct, but he was interrupted by
the arrival of William. He entered, fay-

ing

ing that the villagers, having heard the beauteous lady they had feen was the Countefs, were very unwilling to go without being permitted to fee her again, and very earneftly entreated fhe would let them pay their duty to her, if it were but for a moment. Caroline, led by Walftein, defcended into the court, and was received with redoubled cries of *" Life! Happinefs and long life, to my Lord and my Lady!"* The Count ordered wine and money to be diftributed, and Caroline, clafping his hand, moft affectionately, whifpered, "thefe good people, my Walftein, know not that they really celebrate our bridal day, the epocha of happinefs confirmed!—Would you but permit"—

"Permit, Caroline!—Speak, command."

" See

" See what a number of young people here are. Do you not think there are fome lovers, among them, who wifh to marry, but whom poverty keeps afunder? Ah! let us make them as happy as we are ourfelves !"

The Count kiffed her hand with tranf-port.—" Dear, adorable Caroline!—Let us do ftill more; let us perpetuate the memory of this fortunate day, fince it is the day when Caroline is given to my arms. Let us, here, in this fcene of blifs, annually, beftow fix marriage portions, and do thou, my Caroline, inform the good peafants of the inftitution."

Caroline again preffed the hand of Walftein, fpoke to the people, and new acclamations, new benedictions were uttered

with

with redoubled fervency; in the midſt of
theſe tumultuous tranſports, the voices of
young lovers were ſtill louder and more ardent than the others, and their prayers that
God might for ever bleſs their good Lord
and Lady reached the ſkies!

Walſtein, perceiving Louiſa and Juſtin
in one corner of the court, with their little
family, called, and preſented them to Caroline. "Here, my love," ſaid he, "are
ſome good people with whom you are already acquainted." "Ah!" ſaid Caroline, "this is the beauteous Louiſa."—
(Louiſa bluſhed and became more beautiful; for, though childbearing and the du-
ties of her ſtation had ſomewhat faded the
roſes on her cheeks, ſhe ſtill was exceedingly handſome.

"Oh!

" Oh! yes, my Lady," faid Juftin, with his open expreffive countenance, which at once befpoke the capacity of his mind and the honefty of his heart : " You are very right ; this is my beauteous Louifa: there's not a man in the world, 'tis my opinion, has fo handfome a wife, except my Lord the Count ; and that is but juft. It is the recompenfe of heaven for having beftowed Louifa on the poor Juftin."

It was now Caroline's turn to blufh ! She careffed the two boys who were fine little fellows, and, perceiving the pregnancy of Louifa, prevented her petition, by offering, of her own accord, to ftand godmother to the child. Louifa would have knelt at her feet, if Caroline would have fuffered her ; but Juftin nothing could reftrain ; he kiffed the hem of her robe, and,

F 3   rifing,

rifing, faid, "Surely God loves me, for he hears and grants me all my prayers! No fooner did I afk him to give me Louifa than he put it into the heart of my Lord to make her mine; and then I again begged a Louifa for my Lord, and behold he has found one! Well then, I next will pray him to grant my Lady two little boys, as handfome as ours; nay and I have no doubt but they will foon be here."

Caroline turned away, ftooped to the children, and gave each of them a kifs and a ducat, while Walftein, affected, fhook Juftin by the hand, and threw his purfe into his hat. To efcape thanks and prevent the efforts of gratitude, which, when beyond expreffion, are always painful, he afked Caroline to walk in the garden, to which fhe inftantly agreed. It was then

the

the month of December, the air was piercing, the earth covered with snow, and the waters with frost, yet neither frost nor snow were seen, nor was the sharp air felt by Caroline and Walstein. Never did walk in spring appear to them so delicious. Long has it been known that love can embellish all things, and that, where the beloved object is present, there is neither winter nor summer, spring nor fall. Indeed, the gardens were remarkable for their beauty, extent, and the taste with which they were disposed; and, as such, were visited by travellers. Caroline had seen something of them, on her other bridal day, and perhaps more than she saw at present, though she now walked all over them. At length, the Count, fearing the effect of the cold, brought her back to the Chateau. Here they found a collation such as the rustic

hoards

hoards of Louiſa could afford. She had been buſy in providing cream, new cheeſe, cheſnuts, honeycombs, and a part of the kid that Juſtin had killed. "How fortunate it was," ſaid Louiſa, "that I had it ready dreſſed to regale our good old father."

"What Joſſelin!" cried Caroline; "nay then, Louiſa, you muſt go and bring him to eat with us." Louiſa ran to ſeek him, and in the Sire came, ſupported by Juſtin, and tremulous ſtill more with joy than old age. The Count and Caroline roſe, both went to him, and, each taking him by an arm, placed him in a great chair; after which the Count, filling him a bumper, ſaid, "Drink this, my brave Joſſelin, to the health of the happieſt of mortals!"

"And this," ſaid Juſtin, "to him who well deſerves to be the happieſt!"

Joſſelin

Joffelin would have fpoken, but he was fo much affected he could only utter parts of fentences, and raife his hands and eyes to heaven. After, however, having drank a third glafs to the health of my lady the Countefs, and after a long look at her, he fuddenly exclaimed—" Bleffed be God for having made fo beauteous a Lady purpofe- ly for our good Lord! Oh yes! you are beautiful, madam, and very, very good! I can fee, I am fure you are; but you have an angel for a hufband! Did you know what he has done for us, how he preferved, how he provided for, my Louifa!"

And now the good Joffelin, animated by wine, and having once begun to fpeak, was not willing to be filent. He recount- ed the whole hiftory, to Caroline, of the marriage of his daughter; and how he would not hear of Juftin, and how my

Lord

Lord the Count came round him, and how he gave them a good farm, and fifty ducats down, and how he had the misfortune to wound himſelf as he went from their houſe, . and how they carried him on hurdles to the Chateau of Ronebourg; and a thouſand other *bows* which Caroline knew as well as he, yet would ſhe not interrupt him; the pleaſure the old man felt in talking was a pleaſure to Caroline; nay, ſhe even liſtened with delight to this ſimple but natural village eloquence; it flowed pure from the heart and never thought of well-placed words or ſtudied expreſſions; and particularly to the praiſe of Walſtein, which was inceſſantly repeated, and which drew the ſweeteſt tears of ſenſibility to her eyes. She looked up to this dear, this beloved huſband, and ſaw his heart in ſympathy with hers; ſhe ſtretched

out

out her hand to him with a foft fmile, an
expreffion which no words can convey.
Love, virtue, and happinefs were united,
and this fingle moment would have been,
a large compenfation for an age of pain.

Joffelin drank, talked, and became
more and more animated. He fpoke of
his houfe, his family, the care his children
took of him, of his dear Juftin, who was.
the beft of fons, of hufbands, and of fathers. "An it were to do again," faid
he, "I would give him my Louifa if he
were not worth a groat. Not, my Lord,
that your bounty has done any harm. And
then when I fee thefe little urchins, playful, capering round me—Ah! how does
it rejoice my very heart! It makes me
young again; and, if my dear Cicely were
ftill living, I fhould be happier now than

ever

ever——But, pray, my Lord, what is become of our mafter's fon, the young Baron of Lindorf? I can remember him lefs
than either of thefe. Many a time have I
had him in my arms: nay, I am his nurfe
father, and fhall always love him. I was
told he was going to marry the fifter of my
Lord; and right glad we were to hear it;
for fuch honourable noble fouls ought to
marry. Is it true, my Lord? Is he your
brother?"

"Not yet," faid Caroline, rifing, and
returning Louifa's youngeft boy to his mother, whom, till then, fhe had held in her
lap. Juftin and Louifa underftood by this
it was time to retire, and Louifa hinted as
much to her father; but the old man was
fo happy, in his arm chair, with the Count,
the Countefs, and the bottle, that he could

by

by no means refolve to leave them.—" Let me alone, my child," faid he; " it is the happieft day I ever beheld, and, at my time of life, one has not much happinefs to lofe."—" But we are troublefome, father," faid Louifa, " to my Lord the Count." " Not in the leaft, I tell thee; thou art a foolifh girl; I know him better than thou doft; why it is his delight to fee others happy; is it not, my Lord? Am not I right, and is not fhe wrong? But our children, now a days, will be wifer than their fathers."

Walftein fmiled, and Caroline again fat down, and made a fign to Louifa; while the old man, more happy than a monarch, began to fing. He could not finifh his fong. " So it is," faid he, " I am good for nothing now; but I have a heart for

for all that. Ah! madam, if you had but heard me give the word of command! But come, fon Juftin, it is now thy turn. Where is thy flageolet? Play madam a tune. Louifa fhall fing, and the little apes here fhall dance. Pfhaw, what fimpletons you are, you think of nothing: an it were not for me, here would you leave my Lord and Lady to yawn themfelves to fleep."

Caroline having fignified fhe really fhould be glad to hear Juftin play, he took out his flageolet and played fome al- lemandes, to which the little ones danced with much more grace and meaning than could have been expected, while their mother watched every motion, and the old man chuckled as he looked at the Count and Countefs. "Did not I tell you,"

you," faid he, "it was worth your feeing? and now, Louifa, do thou fing the fong thy hufband made a few days ago."

"How!" cried Caroline; "is Juftin a Poet too?"

"No, Madam, no poet." faid Juftin: "I only write a couplet now and then for my Louifa." He then played a wild pleaf-ing melody, by way of fymphony, on his flageolet, and Louifa, with the timid fim-plicity and fweetnefs of the village voice, fung as follows.

The marriage honey moon, they fay,
Grown languid on the marriage day,
   Now fcarce, alas! that day outlives;
But, ah! Louifa, thou doft prove
How little fuch folks know of love,
   Who thus defcribe the joys it gives!

Poor

Poor silly people! Wherefore tire
Of blifs which I fo much admire,
  Tafte each returning day fo pure;
And, feeling how I ftill adore,
Still each returning day am more
  Convinc'd it ever fhall endure ?

I hear of kings and mighty men,
I know no kings, and, therefore, can
  No fancies form of kingly joys;
But this I know, not lands or towns,
No, I'd not give for globes or crowns
  My dear Louifa and my boys.

Louifa ended, and Juftin laid down his
flageolet. He had fuppofed it poffible
that, as he himfelf loved fo much to hear
his Louifa fing, others might wifh to hear
her fing likewife; forefeeing, therefore, this
occafion, and overflowing with gratitude
at the return of his Lord, while the Count
and Caroline had walked into the garden,
Juftin, anxious to make this gratitude
                                        known,

known, had compoſed the following ſtanza,
which, modeſtly advancing a few ſteps,
he himſelf now ſung.

Ah ! might my artleſs ſong but ſhow
How much to my kind Lord I owe ;
    Might I but half I feel impart ;
I then, to all my former ſtore,
Should add one grateful pleaſure more,
    And eaſe my now half burſting heart.

Juſtin ſung with as much feeling as he
wrote, and the Count and Caroline, affected and aſtoniſhed at his talents, gave him
all the praiſe he merited. The modeſt
and the ſimple Juſtin ſaid it was Louiſa
who had taught him every thing, for had
it not been for the pleaſure he took in
pleaſing her he ſhould have known nothing. " But," ſaid Caroline, " have you
compoſed this laſt ſtanza inſtantly, and
without having thought on it before ?"—
                              " Not

" Not entirely," replied Juftin ; " though I do think, my Lady, I could undertake, ay and perform too, a more difficult thing for my Lord the Count."

The heart of Caroline was full, or rather overflowing. During the fong, the good Joffelin had fallen afleep, but his children awaked him fufficiently to get him away, and as foon as Caroline was alone with the Count fhe gave vent to the fweeteft tears fhe had ever fhed. The old man, the happy couple, the veneration and love they all had for the Count, which extended itfelf to her, had all together fuch an effect upon her feelings, and imagination, that her hufband appeared a fupernatural being, a benevolent Deity, whom it was her duty to adore, and whom, in reality, adore fhe did. As foon as her mind was a little calm, " permit me, my dear Lord," faid fhe, " to afk

you

you the same question that Josselin asked some time since. Will not Lindorf become our brother?"

" Would to Heaven he might," answered the Count; " but you forget, my love"——

" What ?"

" That it is not Matilda, now, who could make Lindorf happy."

" And why not ?"

" Because, for some months, he was in love with Caroline of Lichtfield."

" But that Caroline no longer exists; he will never see her more; in her stead he will find Caroline of Walstein, who never can inspire any thing but fraternal friendship,

ſhip, which cannot any way impede his love for Matilda. Let him but ſee her, once again, and he himſelf will not be able to comprehend how he might, for a moment, forget her. I wiſh I were certain that Matilda's affections have undergone no change; there is a word in one of your letters which gave me a little uneaſineſs. Do you ſuſpect ſhe does not love Lindorf, and that the Baron de Zaſtrow"——Walſtein ſmiled, preſſed the hand of Caroline, and interrupted her by taking out his pocketbook and giving Caroline the laſt letter he had received from Matilda to read——And, Oh! how much affected was ſhe as ſhe read! How often did ſhe repeat, "Dear girl! Charming Matilda! Lovely Siſter! Yes, thou ſhalt live with us, ſhalt regain thy lover, thy brother, and the tendereſt of friends. But why," added ſhe, as ſhe returned the

letter

letter to the Count, "did not you, my Lord, immediately fly to Drefden, to give aid and eafe to this dear Sifter?"

"I will tell you why, my love—My Caroline was dying, and while fhe was in danger could I leave her?"

"Well, but you anfwered Matilda's letter?"

"I did; though, at prefent, I wifh I had not; and confefs I begin to be uneafy at her filence."

"Good Heaven! How you muft have grieved her! Dear Matilda!"——Then, fuddenly rifing, Caroline, with clafped hands and ardent impetuofity, went up to the Count, and, with a tone of moft earneft fupplication, added, "My dear, dear Lord, let me beg, let me conjure you, not

to

to refuse me the favour I am about to afk. Let us depart to-morrow morning for Drefden, to relieve Matilda; I burn to be acquainted, to live with her, to give her confolation, and, I hope, happinefs. Only read her letter again, and you cannot have the leaft hefitation. She is now, perhaps, in tears, is this moment in dif- trefs, when I am fo happy; and I myfelf am the caufe of her affliction! And have I, then, dear Matilda, have I robbed thee of thy lover, and deprived thee of thy bro- ther? Oh! how many wrongs have I done thee! No, no, never, never fhall I be truly at eafe, till I fee thee as bleft as I myfelf am." Caroline fpoke with fo much energy, her eyes and features expreffed fo well her fenfations, and fhe herfelf was fo beautiful, that Walftein fell involuntarily on his knee before her, where he long remained with

his

his lips fixed on her hand, without the power to anfwer a word—" Tell me, my Lord," added fhe, with earneftnefs, " fhall we, are we to depart to-morrow ?"

" Lovely, adorable Caroline !" cried the Count, " how well thou knoweft my heart ! My abfence from my fifter, and the apprehenfion that fhe may be unhappy, were the only things that could poffibly interrupt my prefent felicity; but to leave you, Caroline, or to propofe a journey in the depth of winter, and during fuch fevere weather, was more than I could undertake."

" Nay, my Lord, now you furely joke. I thought it was always fine weather when one went in fearch of a friend in the company of a lover. We fhall pafs through Potfdam: fhall you fee the King ?"

" By

" By all means, my love; it is a duty I cannot neglect; and, if I might venture, I would afk, in my-turn, whether Caroline would "———Caroline perfectly underflood the Count, and blufhed; fhe had not feen the King fince the day of her nup- tials, which was now above a year; and, feeling how much caufe he had to be dif- fatisfied with her conduct, fhe trembled at the thought of being prefented. While fhe was laft at Berlin, her mourning and her health were fufficient pretexts to obtain delay, and the Count, we have feen, had his reafons for wifhing to indulge her in this delay. At prefent, he perceived her inquietude, and flopped fhort; but fhe, immediately 'recovering herfelf, anfwered, with an enchanting fmile, " It is high time, my Lord, is it not, I fhould no longer re- main fo childifh ?———Well, lead me, take me to him; I will kneel at his feet; I

fuppofe

fuppofe he will fcold me; he will do very right; for I have well deferved his anger; but, when he has ended, I, however, will fcold him in my turn."

"You! my angel."

"Yes, I; and very feverely, too, for having figned that dreadful paper, this morning."

Each word Caroline uttered tranfported the Count with happinefs and love, even to intoxication, difpelling every fhadow of remaining doubt, if doubt might remain after the frank and natural manner in which fhe had fpoken of Lindorf, and her defire to fee him and Matilda united. But, no, Walftein had no doubts; the ingenuous and affectionate Caroline knew not diffi-

VOL. III.　　　G　　　　mulation;

mulation; fhe expreffed her feelings too forcibly, and with a conviction that deceit cannot affume. Had fhe been filent, indeed, her eyes, her fmiles, the pleafure painted in her countenance, would all have fpoken: her lips knew not falfehood, and her features were the organs of a pure and angelic foul. When Caroline faid *I love*, no proteftations, no vows, were wanting; and this fhe had faid fo often, during the courfe of that fortunate, that blifsful day, that the Count might well remain perfuaded of her truth.——They fupped on the kid that Juftin had killed fo a-propos; for, the Count, when he fet off in the morning, was too deeply afflicted to think of food; and this fimple repaft was the moft delicious either of them had ever made. Our hiftory does not inform us whether long habit made the Count, as

ufual,

ufual, leave Caroline's apartment after
fupper; the reader muft, therefore, fuppofe what he pleafes on that fubject: but,
in the morning, Caroline made the Count
promife they fhould foon return to this
charming eftate; ", for," added fhe, with a
foftened voice and downcaft eyes, "I fhall
love it as long as I live!"

In proportion as they drew near to Potfdam, the fears of Caroline augmented;
this the Count perceived, and endeavoured
to infpire her with fortitude. He related
a thoufand traits of the King's goodnefs to
him, "who," faid he, "is more than my King,
he is my friend. Yes, dear Caroline, it is
to my friend I am going to prefent one who
will make life a continued dream of felicity, and one whom I received from himfelf. Had you heard him yefterday morning, how long he perfifted to refufe the

cruel

cruel favour I came to beg, and when, at laft, he yielded to my perfecutions and figned that fatal paper, had you feen him return it to me, you would have no fears. " Reflect, think again, dear Walftein," faid he. " I am truly grieved at your determination. I wifhed to make you happy, and ftill I think you might be fo; it is with infinite regret I have figned the paper, and I fincerely hope you will make no ufe of it." Such, Caroline, is the monarch who foon is to be a witnefs of the felicity of his friend."

By this time they were in the court of the palace, and the Count, alighting, left Caroline in the carriage. The King, according to his cuftom, was mounting his horfe to ride round the fort and exercife his troops. He perceived Walftein and ftopped——" Ah ! are you there, Count ?" faid said he; "I am glad to fee you; I thought of you all yefterday, and, though I faw the High Chamberlain, did not mention a word of what has paffed. Do not be rafh, let me, myfelf, fpeak to Caroline. I fcarcely can confent"———

"My gracious Sovereign, fhe is here!"

"Who?"

"Caroline! My wife! My lovely, my adored wife! The wife your Majefty be-ftowed on me, and who is now more be-loved, more dear than ever!"

"Are you in your fenfes, Walftein?"

"Perfectly, Sir; it was yefterday morn-ing that I was frantic; but Caroline has reftored me to reafon, life, and blifs! She

loves

loves me, wishes to be mine, and once more I throw myself at your Majesty's feet to beg her as the greatest of all blessings your royal bounty could grant!"

Yes, the Count was kneeling to the King; who, himself, not perfectly under-standing how a woman might be the cause of all this delirium, laughed, bade him " rise and explain." The Count obeyed; related the despair of Caroline, her arrival at Walstein, their present intended journey to Dresden, for which he now asked the King's permission, and, afterwards, ear-nestly entreated his Majesty's confirmation of their union before their departure. Both were willingly granted, and the Monarch himself went up to Caroline, who was still waiting in her carriage till the Count's re-turn. She was a great deal affected at seeing the King approach, and would have

descended

defcended from the coach, but the King
faid to her, " Stay where you are, Lady
Walftein, ftay where you are; all is well;
forget what is paft. I am fatisfied, live
happy, and let me have as many fubjects
as poffible like yourfelves. Walftein,
make no delay, depart, return as foon as
you can, and bring with you the lovely
Matilda." His Majefty then took the
Count by the hand, faluted Caroline, and
left them both exceedingly moved by
his benevolent condefcenfion, a favor Kings
are fo feldom difpofed to beftow. They
fet off immediately for Berlin, made preparations for their journey, and were foon
on their road to Dreiden, anticipating the
mutual pleafure the meeting with Matilda
would occafion. The Count forefaw many
difficulties which might arife from his aunt
and young de Zaftrow, but was deter-

mined

mined to overcome them all, and bring
Matilda to Berlin. He concealed his fears
from Caroline, whofe hopes ran high and
happinefs was great, in thinking fhe fhould
gain a fifter and a friend. We have before
related how defirous fhe was of a bleffing
fo neceffary and fo precious; and to have
the fifter of Walftein for this friend, with
whom fhe might converfe, while he was
abfent, of all her paft and prefent feelings,
certain of being heard with an intereft almoft equal to her own, was to double this
bleffing.

To love is not fufficient; friendfhip, to
whom love may unbofom itfelf, is alfo
neceffary; and Caroline, already, felt the
delicious tranfports of telling Matilda how
dearly fhe loved her brother. In this their
impatience, for the Count was as defirous

as Caroline of being at Dresden, they travelled the two first days with all possible
speed, making no stay, by day, except to
change horses, and at night only taking
two or three hours repose. But the strength
of Caroline by no means equalled her
wishes, and the second evening she found
herself so fatigued she was obliged, when
they came to a small village, to entreat the
Count would go no farther that night.
Walstein, it may well be supposed, readily
consented; but, suspecting the accommo-
dations would not be very good, he sent
a servant before to procure a bed. At
last, they were met, at the end of the village, by the servant, and the landlord of
a small, indifferent inn. Our host, judg-
ing, by the attendants, his guests were
great people, and fearing to lose the promised harvest, came himself, to make it

the

the more secure. He had only two bed-chambers, each with two beds, and both thése were in the possession of a young gentleman and his lady, who had arrived the evening before. The husband had a wound in his arm, which, by the motion of the carriage, had been opened; and this was likely to detain him some days longer; for which reason, to make certain of the two chambers, he had paid for them before-hand. This, however, did not much em-barrass our host, who was a merry, un-polished, country fellow.

"I warrant me," said he, "they will let you have one of the chambers, for what occa-sion have they for two? They are so loving, and so handsome, that they are never asunder all day; and why may they not as well be together all night? No, no; they will not be vexed at that."

The

The hoft kept talking till they came to the inn, but the Count, however, thought it neceffary to go himfelf, and entreat the ftrangers to fuffer the Countefs to lie in one of the beds. Meanwhile the hoftefs fhewed Caroline into her own chamber. The Count went up a dark ftair-cafe, and wanted the landlord to introduce him; but he, little ufed to the forms of good breeding, led him into a kind of entry, at the far end of which was a door open, and, telling the Count he would find them there, left him to introduce himfelf.

Walftein advanced, and faw a young lady, at the farther part of the chamber, elegantly dreffed, and tying a black fcarf round the neck of a young gentleman, fo as to fupport his arm. As her white and charming hand paffed his cheek he em-

G 6   ployed

ployed his other arm to feize and kifs it
'with rapture.   The picture was interefting,
and the Count durft not difturb the young
couple, whom he filently beheld, remem-
bering his own happinefs.   Fearing to be
thought rude, after ftanding a moment,
he was going to retire; but the young lady,
happening to look towards the door, faw
him, gazed for a moment, flew to him
with open arms, and, with aftonifhment
in her countenance, exclaimed, "It is my
brother! my dear dear brother!"   .

Lindorf (Yes! it was Lindorf himfelf!)
forgot his wound, and inftantly rofe——
"Heavens! Is it poffible! Can it be Walftein?"——Walftein it was, and Lindorf
preffed him to his bofom; while Matilda,
hanging round his neck, kiffed and kiffed,
and knew not whether to weep or dance
for joy.

Need

Need we fay the Count was aftonifhed?—
Matilda and Lindorf! His fifter and his
friend both in his arms! Had his fenfes
refufed belief his heart would have convinced him it was truth; and, though
unable to comprehend by what miracle
he might find two fuch people in fuch a
place, he, neverthelefs, yielded to all the
tranfport the prodigy infpired. For fome
time, Lindorf! Matilda! Brother! Sifter!
Friend! Interjections and exclamations
only were uttered, only were heard—The
Count added the name of Caroline, and, at
length, faid, " fhe is here, dear Matilda,
here, with me, let us go to her."

" Here! Caroline here! My fifter here!"
cried Matilda.

Light and fwift as the young greyhound
at his returning mafter's voice, Matilda
flies down ftairs and already is in the arms

of

of Caroline, who, prefently, knew her;
more, indeed, from her affectionate careffes,
and the repeated epithet of "dear dear fifter,"
than from the portrait of Lindorf. The
gentlemen followed, and the furprife of
Caroline increafed; but furprife and pleafure of the pureft nature were her only fenfations. Lindorf is her brother, and her
friend, and fhe hefitates not to kifs him
with that frank and natural tendernefs by
which true and fimple friendfhip fo well
is characterized. " And may I, then, call
you brother?" faid fhe; " may I tell you
I love you? Oh! yes, I know not how
much I fhall love the hufband of my dear
Matilda, and the friend of my dear, dear,
dear Walftein!"

This open ingenuous manner would
have taught Lindorf, had he himfelf been
infenfible of, his duty. He certainly feared

to

to meet Caroline : the scenes that had so
lately passed could not be totally oblite-
rated from his imagination; but the manner in which she received him, the tone
of voice in which she uttered those few
words, in the presence of Walstein and
Matilda, wholly deprived him of all dread,
either of himself or her. He was surprised to find that the redoubted Caroline
was no more than the wife of his friend,
and the sister of Matilda; and for whom
he felt no sensations beyond these tranquil
and legitimate bounds—"Yes," answered
he, with fortitude and enthusiasm, "yes,
Caroline, I am your brother, your friend,
the friend of Walstein, and I feel myself
worthy of these titles, which are become
so dear, so inestimable!" Then, seizing the
hand of Matilda—"Dear Count," said he,
"you invited me to return, and promised
me happiness. Here, as the ultimate hap-

piness

pinefs to which I afpire, let me receive this hand, which once was promifed me from my Walftein : I think my future life will prove I know its value."

The Count was not long in confidering an anfwer, and his reply was accompanied with an earneft wifh to hear what ftrange circumftances had united them; if they were yet married; what had occafioned the wound of Lindorf; where they were going, whence they came; and, in fine, the full explanation of what, at prefent, feemed fo wholly enigmatical. We are not without our hopes that the reader, in fome degree, participates the Count's curiofity; and that he now imagines himfelf in the ruftic chamber of a ruftic inn, in company with four perfons, the moft happy the earth contained, feeling all that love and fweet friendfhip can feel, feated round an antique chimney,

chimney, speaking all at once, and each asking a thousand questions without waiting for a single reply.

And now behold the lovely Matilda weeping and laughing both at once, kissing her brother, embracing Caroline, holding out one hand to her dear Lindorf, and then, suddenly, with a mighty grave face, and serious tone, commanding silence! "Yes, silence! For one full quarter of an hour, I impose silence on you all," said she, seating herself erect; "for, I assure you, I am not a little vain of having a story to relate. It is almost as singular," said she to her brother, "as the fine tales you used to tell me when I was a very little, little girl."—Silence being thus obtained, and the eyes of the company fixed on Matilda, she, addressing herself to the Count, thus began.

"There

"There was a bird-catcher"——

" A bird-catcher!" exclaimed they all at once.

" Yes, a bird-catcher," replied fhe, with great gravity. " Before I begin my hiftory I firft intend to relate a little fable and put a queftion to my brother. Do not be impatient, I fhall foon have done—There was once a bird-catcher who, by his tricks and artifices, enticed a poor little bird into his nets. Ah! how wretched was that poor little bird! How did it beat its wings in its confinement, and call all its friends to its affiftance! But the bird-catcher took care not one of them fhould hear its cries. At laft came a linnet, and flew round the net in which it was entangled. "Poor little bird," faid the linnet, "thou wouldeft lament

ftill

ftill louder if thou kneweft all the mifchief that awaits thee. To-morrow they will clip thy wings, for ever deprive thee of thy liberty, fhut thee up in a cage with a bird thou doft not love, and for ever prevent thy meeting the mate thou haft left at freedom in the groves." Then did the little bird, at hearing this, cry ftill louder; and the linnet was fo moved that it faid, " Let us try if there are no means to fave thee." Whereupon they both began to peck at the threads of the net, and crack, by and by, one of them was broken; fo that the little bird got firft its head out, next one of its wings, at laft both, fpread them, vaulted aloft in air, and flew, right joyous, again to find its friends and former happinefs.

" And now tell me, dear brother, whether

ther was the bird-catcher, who thus tried to deprive the poor little bird of its liberty, or the poor little bird, that endeavoured to regain this liberty, wrong?"

" The bird-catcher," my dear girl, cried the Count, enchanted at the art, simplicity, and grace, she had mingled in her apologue. " The charming little bird will never be wrong if it appeals to me; for I am certain my heart will approve what even my reason may condemn."

Matilda, instantly, clasped the neck of Walstein, and, with tears of joy, exclaimed; " I have found my brother; he is still the same, ever benevolent and ever good, and I no longer dread either his reproaches or my own. Surely, I did right in quitting those malicious people who made me doubt his friendship."

" Doubt

" Doubt my friendſhip! Dear Matilda,
let me beg you to explain your meaning."

" Yes," continued ſhe, with vivacity,
" they have had the cruelty to ſay, nay even
to prove, you no longer loved me, wrote
to me no longer, and would ſee me no
more; that you forbad me to think of
Lindorf, commanded me to marry the Baron de Zaſtrow, had departed for Ruſſia,
and, in fact, that I had no longer any brother, for it was the ſame thing."

Matilda could not proceed, and the
tears ran down her lovely roſy cheeks; yet,
while ſhe wept ſhe ſmiled: it was a ſum-
mer ſhower which refreſhens nature and
inſpires new pleaſure.

" What a child am I!" ſaid ſhe; " I
knew

knew it was all falfe; I enjoy your company, here you are, you love me, and yet
you fee the fuppofition makes me weep;
but no, I will laugh; and now—there, now
will. I relate the full and whole hiftory of
the poor little bird."

Before fhe began, the Count afked feveral queftions concerning what they had
told her againft him, and found his aunt
had intercepted and concealed the letter in
which he had promifed his fifter foon to
come to Drefden, and fet her free. She
managed fo as to make Matilda believe the
Count had written to her, his aunt. His
wifh that fhe might marry the Baron de
Zaftrow was changed into a pofitive command, and the voyage of Lindorf into England was a love affair, and a project of marriage with an Englifh lady. The letter of

the

the Count, inftead of Ronebourg, was dated at Peterfburg; and the innocent Matilda, being fhewn her brother's hand-writing, was the dupe of all thefe artifices. The arrival of the Count, it is true, would foon undeceive her; but they hoped to have Matilda married before that hap-pened, and, fince the Count had wifhed, he certainly would eafily be brought to pardon the marriage.

Had Matilda been of a lefs determined character her aunt would, no doubt, have obtained her end; but fhe found an oppo-fition, a fortitude which nothing could fhake. It feemed inconceivable to young de Zaftrow; for never, till then, had he fuppofed it poffible to refift the elegance, the graces, and the charms he had acquired in his travels. A year's refidence

at

at Paris, his acquaintance with certain noble and fashionable gamesters there, and his success with actresses, who had made most heavy demands on his purse, had so fully convinced him of his irresistible merit, that he had imagined nothing more was necessary, in order to conquer, than to appear. To his aunt he left the care of courtship, and thought Matilda had every right to yield when he had declared, upon his honour, she was as handsome as an angel; that her shape was quite charming; that there was something of a French cast in her countenance; that she was almost as desirable as Mademoiselle du Thé, of the Opera house; that she sung nearly as well as Mademoiselle du Gazon, of the *Theâtre Italien*; and that, when she was his wife, he would incontinently take her to Paris, where there was no doubt but she would

strike.

ſtrike. All which he ſaid looking at himſelf in the glaſs, admiring his leg, diſplay-
ing the brilliant on his finger, and, occa-
ſionally, interrupting himſelf to expatiate
on the merits of certain faſhionable bau-
bles he had brought from France.

" Such," ſaid Matilda, " is the being
with whom my aunt is ſo enraptured ; to
whom ſhe was determined to marry me ;
and of whoſe perſon, wit, and paſſion, ſhe
was continually vaunting. I own that, for
my part, I could ſee nothing but a very fair
complexioned, very mincing, very delicate,
very vain, very ſelf-ſufficient young gentleman ; who loved only one perſon in the
whole world, himſelf, and who only did
me the honour to think of me becauſe I
was the ſiſter of the King's favourite, and
the heireſs of Madam de Zaſtrow. I by

Vol. III.   H   no

no means endeavoured to conceal my thoughts, concerning either him or Lindorf, from my aunt; she well knew I disliked the one as much as I loved the other, and her whole endeavour was to make me reverse this manner of thinking.—" You see," said she, " your brother has changed his opinion."—" Yes, madam," answered I, " but his opinion has not changed my heart."—" Your Lindorf no longer loves you"—" And must I punish myself for his infidelity?"—"You will never see him again."—" I may love him, neverthelefs, and keep my promife."—" But his inconftancy releafes you"—" Not in the leaft; his inconftancy releafes himfelf, but if I am not inconftant is that my fault? Or can he, or you, or I myfelf, or any other being in the world, make me forget to love him and teach me to love another?" (What did Lindorf feel as thus Matilda fpoke?)

" Thefe

" Thefe cconverfations ufually ended in ill-humour. I was, by turns, fcolded, careffed, flattered, and menaced ; and, notwithftanding all my firmnefs, was almoft driven to defpair. At length, I determined to write ; not to you, brother, for I fuppofed you ftill in Ruffia, and they might have married me again and again before I could receive your anfwer; befide I was fomewhat piqued at your neglect and filence ; therefore, I fay, once more, not to you but—to Lindorf I wrote."

" To Lindorf ! In England ! How did you know his addrefs ?"

" Know ! I knew not, perfectly, if he were there ; for I fometimes would flatter myfelf they had been telling me falfehoods; though many circumftances led me to

think

think he was, and I wrote. Writing was a momentary eafe and confolation, and, though my letter remained in my pocket-book after it was written, I ftill imagined myfelf lefs unhappy. I had fome fmall hopes of difcovering if Lindorf really were in England, and, perhaps, of remitting him this letter, and you fhall hear on what thefe hopes were founded.

"When I arrived at Drefden, Mademoifelle de Manteul, an amiable girl, but fomewhat older than I, had been exceedingly polite to me, and the intimacy of the family at my aunt's occafioned me to fee her often. She long had loft her mother, and lived with an old gouty father and younger brother; therefore, enjoyed a liberty which rendered her houfe and acquaintance exceedingly agreeable, and fhe

was,

was, continually, either with me or invit-
ing me to vifit her.

" Flattered by the friendfhip of a young
lady of five and twenty, I returned her
politenefs, and we became as familiar as
circumftances would permit. Somewhat
timid, on account of the difference of our
age, which fhe, however, endeavoured to
make me forget, I, though moft defirous
of a confidante, durft not tell her the fecret
of my heart. She had a kind of—of for-
wardnefs in her manner, owing to her education, and was, likewife, moft intimate
with my aunt, to whom fhe affiduoufly paid
her court ; befide which fhe had an evident partiality in favour of the Baron de
Zaftrow, fo that I feared making an additional enemy, inftead of a friend. I could
with much greater eafe have confided my

thoughts

thoughts to her brother, whofe age was nearer my own, and whofe mild yet manly character might render him more indul-gent ; but he, alfo, was the friend of the young Baron, and, indeed, rather feemed to avoid than to feek being alone with me, and it was not long before he informed us he was going to travel for fome years.

"Oh ! how did my heart palpitate when I heard England was to be the firft country he vifited ! How then did I wifh to tell him my fecret, entreat him to feek out Lindorf, and conjure him to take charge of my letter ! But no opportunity could I find. He was too bufy in preparing for his departure, and feemed forrowful at being obliged to leave Drefden and his fa-mily. I feldom faw him, and, when I did, found myfelf abafhed. If ever I approached,

with

with intent to fpeak of his voyage to England, and to add a word relative to what
lay neareft to my heart, I trembled, knew
not what to fay, and remained filent; blufh-
ing as if I had fpoken, or as if the whole
world had read my thoughts. Mademoifelle de Manteul was generally a third perfon, and, feeing my embarraffment, increafed it by her pleafantries.

"At length, this brother departed,
while I ftill was feeking the means to in-
duce him to take my letter and give it to
Lindorf; and I was left in the utmoft defpair at having miffed fo favourable an opportunity.

"One refource ftill remained; my friend
might fend it to her brother. But then it
was neceffary to make a full confeffion, and

intereft

intereſt her in the ſuccefs of my paſſion. The better to lead to this I continually ſpoke of England, her brother, the letters ſhe would receive from him, and the dear pleaſure of having a correſpondence with a perſon one loves, though I yet had not dared to pronounce the name of Lindorf. She came to me one morning, and threw a letter into my lap. " There," ſaid ſhe ; " you who think it ſo ſweet a pleaſure to receive letters ; I make you a preſent of that, which, indeed, ought to have been addreſſed to you ; for my brother, though he has written to me, has ſpoken only of you."

" Of me !"

" Yes, of you, little witch. You are the cauſe of his abſence, you have robbed me

of

of my brother; read, read, and return it quickly."

"Nothing of what this meant could I comprehend; but, beginning to read, was soon better instructed. The poor youth had spoken to his sister of sentiments which I neither suspected nor could return, and for which I was much afflicted, and, therefore, would not have read beyond the first page. But, Oh! what a pleasure was I about to deprive myself of! My friend obliged me to go on, and I turned over with vexation and sorrow. Scarcely had I cast my eyes on the second page before I saw, at the bottom, a name !—a name !— Oh! how instantly did grief give way to pleasure, to joys the most ecstatic! It was the name so dear to my heart, so ever present to my thoughts; yes, it was the name

H 5   of

of Lindorf; *the Baron of Lindorf, Captain of the Guards.*

* No deception is there; it is he, he himself, and already have I read every ſyllable, have uttered a hundred exclama-tions, have preſſed the letter to my lips, to my boſom, and have wept and laughed as if I had had no witneſs of my raptures, folly, and frenzy. Looking up, however, and ſeeing the aſtoniſhed air of Mademoi-felle de Manteul, I ran into her arms, and hid my emotion in her boſom. Gently raiſing, ſhe aſked me what it meant. "Matilda!" ſaid ſhe; "my dear Matilda! Why are you thus overjoyed? What is it that thus can agitate you?"

"Ah! read, read—read yourſelf," ſaid I, pointing to a certain paſſage in the letter;

letter; "this will be my explanation;" and while she read, again I hid my face in her bosom.

"I have had the happiness," said M. de Manteul to his sister, "to meet with the "Baron of Lindorf, at Hamburg, a cap- "tain of the Prussian guards, and hope "we shall become intimate friends. We "have been shipmates together, and lodge "in the same house. We are seldom "asunder, our tempers and dispositions "accord wonderfully, for he, like me, is "melancholy, apt to be absent, and re- "grets his country. Without being his "confidant, I dare pronounce his heart is "not more free than mine."

"Ah!" exclaimed I, raising my head and joining my hands, "it is not true,

then,

then, that he loves an Englifh lady, or
that he has been fix months married! My
heart told me it was not!"

" But who, who are you fpeaking of?
Do you know this Baron of Lindorf?"

" Do I know him!"

" Aÿ, do you know him? Do you love
him?"

" Love him! Better than life! Beyond
all thought!"

" And thus, from queftion to queftion,
Mademoifelle de Manteul became the
confidante of all my fecrets, and fully informed of my fituation. I related your
friendfhip, my dear brother, with Lindorf,

dorf, and your defire to fee us united, but, as one muſt always referve a little, of one's wealth for one's felf, I did not tell her that you had changed your opinion; though I let her know my doubts and fears concerning Lindorf, which her filence feemed to confirm. Yet was it poffible, and I endeavoured to perfuade myfelf it was true, that the difficulty of conveying his letters to me was the reafon why I received none. My brother was no longer in his intereſt; he, no doubt, knew it, and that *melancholy*, that *abfent air*, his *regrets for his country*, and his *enſlaved heart*, had each made its impreffion, and re-animated all my hopes.

" My friend had liſtened with an evident concern, and, when I had ended, affectionately kiffing me, faid, " My poor, dear

dear Matilda, why did you not tell me all this fooner? How great would have been the pleafure of the confidence you have refufed me!"

"I feared left you fhould take the part of young de Zaftrow."

"Me! Oh, no!—So far from that I perfectly approve your refiftance, and am only afraid left you fhould yield at laft."

"Never! Never!—While I live, never will I love man but Lindorf!"

"Add, alfo, none other you ought to love; for, in reality, you are as much betrothed as if actually married, and to efpoufe another would be guilt, perjury."

I   "It

" It would, it would !"

" But what is Lindorf doing in England ?"

" Alas ! I know not ; cannot comprehend. I have not heard from him thefe
fix months !"

" And why do you not write ?"

" I have written."

" And where is your letter ?"

" In my pocket-book."

" Mademoifelle de Manteul burft into
a laugh. " It muft produce wonderful
effects," faid fhe, " while it remains there.
Oh ! what a child you are ! Give me your
letter,

letter, and your lover shall have it in a week."—How did I kiss Mademoiselle de Manteul!—And yet her brother's love of me somewhat damped my joy; though I admired his sister's goodness, thus to sacrifice his interests to mine. I was even fearful of abusing it, and shewed some hesitation.—" The task," said she, " I own, is a little cruel; but we must cure him, and this I think will be an infallible means. Give me the letter."—And soon the letter was taken from my pocket-book and in her hand: It was sealed.—" You positively promise, my friend," said she, as she received it, " to be only Lindorf's; never to marry de Zastrow ?"

" Positively! Positively!"

" Very well, that will set my conscience at ease; for I now shall be serving a per-

secuted,

fecuted, married pair. Leave the manage-
ment of every thing to me. We muſt
gain time till you can receive an anſwer,
and take care to leave me with the young
Baron as often as poſſible. I will flatter
and coax him, and thus relieve you from
the pain of practiſing deceit."

"Oh! I cannot deceive. I have always told him, and always ſhall tell him,
I will love none but Lindorf."

" And what is his anſwer?"

" That he has no faith in eternal conſtancy."

" He has not! I underſtand him. But
we will prove what women are capable of;
ſhall we not, my dear Matilda?"

" I moſt

" I moſt ſincerely promiſed we would, and left her, more than ever determined on unſhaken conſtancy and reſiſtance."

Walſtein here ſmiled, and whiſpered ſomething to Lindorf, which the latter returned with like ſignificance. The ladies, and eſpecially Matilda, deſired to know what they ſaid.—" Oh! I promiſe you, you ſhall know by and by; but go on, my dear girl, with your ſtory. You were telling us of the tender friendſhip of Mademoiſelle de Manteul."—" I was," replied Matilda, with ardour; " and never, perhaps, was friendſhip like hers; as you would have ſaid, had you heard her ſpeak, ſeen her eagerneſs, and her zeal. You would have ſuppoſed the ſecret hers, and that her happineſs, not mine, was at ſtake. Every means did ſhe take

to ·

to increafe my fortitude. I might, perhaps, have fufpected myfelf; but my friend
was five and twenty, was therefore prudent,
and, certainly, would not give me ill
counfel. Determined, therefore, with all
poffible obftinacy, not to yield, I waited,
but not with dread, for the anfwer of Lindorf; perfuaded he would tell me truth,
and, if I found I was no longer beloved,
my refolution was taken."

" Why, what would you have done ?"
faid Caroline, with vivacity.

" Every thing I could to have forgotten
him; but, at the fame time, have kept
the vow I made, never to marry, never to
truft a perfidious fex, capable of loving
twice."

This

This was very innocently faid, but it was a dagger to the feeling heart of Caroline. !She blufhed exceffively, caft her fine eyes on the ground, half looked up at Walftein, and, as inftantly, again, looked down. He faw her charming confufion, enjoyed it for a moment, tenderly kiffed her hand, then, addreffing himfelf to Lindorf, faid, "You, my friend, no doubt, approve. Matilda's mode of thinking, and, perhaps, you are right; but each perfon has his opinion. I think nothing can be more flattering than to be the fecond object of the attachment of a delicate and tender heart; and I fhould think this attachment more durable, and more certain, than that of a heart that never had occafion to fufpect and be aware of itfelf."

"How!"

"How!" exclaimed Matilda; "does my brother Walftein preach inconftancy?"

"I do not think a fecond paffion deferves the name, and I only admit of being twice in love."

"Aha! No oftener?"

"No, certainly; no oftener;" faid Caroline, faintly, and preffing the hand o Walftein to her bofom.

"Well, for my part," replied Matilda; "I find the firft time once too often, and that women are very filly creatures ever to love, fince love has fo many pangs for them and fo few for the men. Here was this good gentleman amufing himfelf, in all tranquillity, at London,
while

while I was scolded, persecuted, and despairing from morning till night——(Lindorf with a look petitioned mercy; Matilda smiled and continued.)—I found myself, however, much less unhappy since I had gained a friend to whom I might tell all my griefs; and this friend was so kind, understood so well all my feelings, approved so highly of my love and constancy, and spoke so well of Lindorf, and so ill of de Zastrow, that my obligations were infinite. Nay she was even complaisant enough to admit his visits and endure his conversations, for whole hours, to serve me, and advised me to invite him to come on those evenings I was to visit her. "That will be the means of amusing him and not exposing yourself," said she; "and, likewise, of pleasing your aunt. I promise never to leave you; for,

indeed,

indeed, there is nothing I would not do to ferve you."

"My aunt now became very good humoured, teized me no more, and I hoped, thus, to gain time; but it is now three days fince fhe brought me two large fheets of paper, commanded me to read them, fign which I pleafed, and left me in utter aftonifhment. They feemed like two large contracts! And was I then permitted to chufe between Lindorf and de Zaftrow? Such for a moment were my hopes; but I foon faw they both related to the odious de Zaftrow, whom I hated more and more. One of them was what I had fufpected, a marriage contract with him, to which nothing was wanting but my fignature, and by which I was made heirefs to my aunt. The other was

a deed

a deed of conveyance of this inheritance to
the Baron de Zaftrow, fhould I refufe to
fign the firft.   Oh! how happy was I thus
to be left to my choice! How inftantly
did I fign the conveyance, and run with it,
joyoufly fkipping, into my aunt's apartment!
Her nephew was with her. " There, there,
there !" faid I ; " it is done ; I have figned
it, moft willingly."   Young de Zaftrow,
as vain and felf-fufficient as ever, had not
the leaft doubt but it was the marriage
contract, and, kneeling, returned me a
thoufand thanks for my condefcenfion. " I
am quite delighted, Sir," faid I, laughing,
" to fee you fo pleafed, though, really, you
owe me no thanks, I not having the leaft
merit, for I have only followed my own in-
clinations."

" His tranfports now redoubled, and I
was malicious enough to repeat, with great
                                                    folemnity,

folemnity, " Yes fir, I affure you I have wholly followed my inclination—to remain free.—Befide, my aunt has a right to beftow her benefactions where fhe pleafes; nor have I ever wifhed to enjoy wealth which feems to be put in competition with the greateft of earthly bleffings, the right of beftowing my heart and hand."

" Imagine the look and manner of de Zaftrow as he rofe—My aunt faw which paper it was I had figned, and her eyes fpoke her feelings; but, before fhe had time to give them utterance, I fell, and, kiffing her hands again and again, faid, " My dear, dear aunt, do not be angry ; every thing is well as it is; neither men- tion marriage nor an inheritance which I never defired, nor ever once thought of; only let this contract be deftroyed; (as I

VOL. III. .I ꞇaid

said this I tore it in a thousand pieces)
leave the deed of gift in the possession of
my cousin de Zastrow; men have more
occasion for riches than we have, and I
covet nothing but your friendship, the
friendship of my brother, and the love of
Lindorf, or, at least, the liberty of loving
him all my life. The Baron de Zastrow
will find many women who will be proud
to be distinguished by him, and who will
not be in love with Lindorf; who, therefore, might afford him that happiness I
cannot; and, when you should see your poor
Matilda lying dead of a broken heart,
who, then, could restore her to you?"

"I thought my aunt seemed affected
and was about to yield to my entreaties,
for she tenderly raised me up, pressed my
hand, and, turning towards de Zastrow,
                                        said,

faid, "you hear her, nephew, what do you think?"—De Zaftrow was ftriding furiֹoufly about the chambeֹf. "Think; madam," anfwered he, with a tragic terror in his voice and features, "I cannot think. Death or Matilda muft be mine!" At the fame moment he drew his fword; yes, I affure you, he drew his fword, and feemed determined to kill himfelf. I fprang to him and feized his arm; my aunt cried out like a perfon expiring, and faid fhe was *very very ill!* I knew not which of them to attend, nor could I calm either, till I promifed to do every thing they pleafed; while I myfelf was fo much agitated, and terrified, that I fcarcely could utter thefe few words, which, however, produced an aftonifhing effect. The fword was in its fcabbard again, my aunt came to herfelf, kiffed me, careffed me,

and

and earneftly begged me immediately to
fign.

" Luckily for me, however, I had prevented all figning for that night; as the
torn contract, fcattered about the floor,
informed them. It was, therefore, deferred till the morrow; but they required me
to renew my promife. The moment my
terror was gone, I fhuddered at what had
paffed, and at the engagement I had entered into without knowing what I did;
and when I was defired to confirm this engagement I was fo much affected that I
fainted away. They were obliged to carry
me into my chamber, and lay me on a bed;
the motion fomewhat brought me to myfelf, for, though I could not fpeak, I heard
what they were faying. They thought me
ftill in a fit, and my aunt faid to the Baron,

ron, "Do not be alarmed, nephew, this
will foon be over; we have terrified her a
little too much, but the greateft difficulty
is conquered, fhe has promifed; to-morrow fhe fhall fign, the next day you fhall
marry her, and her brother may then fay
what he pleafes. At prefent we muft leave
her undifturbed."—After which they quitted the chamber, recommending me to the
care of my woman.

"Oh! what infinite matter was here for
reflection, when I came perfectly to myfelf;
which this contributed to effect! I confidered and re-confidered every word, nor
was there one that did not give either furprife, anger, fear, grief, and even joy. I
prefently difmiffed my attendant—*We have
terrified her a little too much!* repeated I.
And fo they have been playing a fcene, in
which I have been the dupe of the comedy!

I 3

A trick,

A trick, concerted between my aunt and this self-killing cousin, to obtain my consent!——I despised the artifice, and, from that moment, held myself free; yet I shrunk back with horror when I recollected *She has promised; to-morrow she shall sign, and the next day you shall marry her*——"No, I will die, first," repeated I. What followed gave me a ray of hope. *Her brother may then say what he pleases——We shall no longer fear him.* "So they stand in awe of this dear brother, then, whom I thought in the interest of my persecutors, but is not! They have deceived me in that too; and I still have a protector, a friend, who will not forsake me."——Alas! in my joy of having again this friend, this good brother, I forgot how far distant we were, and that the next day my fate was to be determined.

"I re-

" I remained thus, agitated by a thoufand different thoughts, when Mademoifelle de Manteul entered. The moment I faw her, I held out my arms, and, weeping, exclaimed, " Oh! come, come to the affiftance of your wretched friend!" Yet little did I imagine all her friendfhip was capable of performing! She was as pale, trembling, and affected as I myfelf—"I know every thing," faid fhe; " I have juft left your aunt. What have you done, Matilda ? You have promifed to marry de Zaftrow."

"He was going to kill himfelf."

" Kill himfelf! filly girl; men are not fo ready to kill themfelves. But what do you mean? Do you intend to keep this fatal promife ? Do you recollect all thofe you have made to Lindorf ?"

I 4 " Ah !

"Ah! can you think I have forgot them?" paffionately anfwered I. "No; they are all engraved on my heart, and ere they are effaced they fhall tear that heart from my bofom! Yet, what am I to do? How may I free myfelf from this detefted marriage? Speak, tell me, dear friend; can you imagine any means of delay till I write to my brother, till he can return and protect me? For, from what I have juft heard, that I now am fure he will. Oh! if he were not in Ruffia, I know what I would do."

"Why, what would you do?" faid Mademoifelle de Manteul, who feemed deep in thought; "what would you do?"

"I would efcape; fly to him for fafety."

"And have you the courage?" faid fhe.
"How

" How I admire you, my young friend !
This is, in reality, the fole means left. I
myfelf thought of it, but durft not make
the propofition."

" Alas !" anfwered I, " the thing is impoffible; my brother is in Ruffia. I never
fhall find the means of going thither."

" I own it is difficult; but have not you
a maternal uncle in London ?"

" I have; my Lord Seymour."

" Suppofe you were to put yourfelf under his protection ?"

" What ! fly to England and Lindorf
there ! Can you imagine"———

" No; I fhould not have imagined that

I 5   would

would have been a reafon to avoid England."

"Ah! my dear friend," faid I, fhaking my head, " if you have no other propofal but this to offer I am undone. Rather would I go to Ruffia, impoffible as it is, and feek an afylum from my brother, than act with fuch imprudence. I fpoke this with fo firm a tone that fhe offered no reply, but afked me what it was *I juft had heard.* I then repeated my aunt's converfation, and, fuddenly interrupting me, fhe exclaimed, " If they have deceived you in one refpect they may have in another, and, it is my firm opinion, your brother is not in Ruffia, for I recollect to have heard fomething as well as you——I will go immediately to your aunt, and, if I am not miftaken, prefently difcover the truth. We then fhall know what we have to do."

" She

" She went, and it was not long before
fhe returned. Pleafure fparkled in her
eyes. " I was right in my conjecture," faid
fhe, as fhe entered ; " they have impofed
upon you; your brother is at Berlin, married to a lovely lady; his letters have been
intercepted, he is foon coming to Drefden,
but they are determined to marry you, with
or without your confent, before his arrival.
To-morrow you will be forced to fign the
contract ; nay, they will even guide your
hand, if you will not fign it willingly, and
the day following you are to be married.
All this has your aunt told me in fecrefy.
" My niece has promifed," faid fhe, " and
fhe fhall keep her promife."

" Oh! my God! my God!" cried I,
" what fhall I do? And you tell me thefe
things with apparent pleafure."

" Why,

" Why, I really thought it would pleafe you to hear your brother is at Berlin, and that you may, if you pleafe, free yourfelf from their tyranny."

" Perhaps I might—but"—

" But——What, and is all your courage gone fo fuddenly ?—Ah ! poor Matilda ; I perceive you never will have the refolution to remain firm. Lindorf has got your letter, is returning, or, perhaps, returned ; and what will he fay when he fhall find you are married ?"

" Cruel friend !" replied I, with chagrin ; " is this your confolation ?"

" What would you have me fay to a fee- ble and timid child, who does not know her own mind ? Thofe evils we want the fortitude

fortitude to rid ourselves of we must endure; and I can assure you that, in two days, if you are at Dresden, you will be the Baroness de Zaftrow."

"Never, never," answered I, with enthusiasm—"Never shall that hated name be mine: I will prove that this feeble and timid child has more resolution than you suspect; nay, has enough to face even death itself."

"Die! Pshaw! Who would die, when they may live, and live happily?"

"I see no means; it is impossible. I cannot go by myself to Berlin. I should lose myself a thousand times; neither should I ever have the strength to get thither."

"Mademoiselle de Manteul could not forbear

bear laughing.—" Poor girl ! And fo you thought I meant to fend you to Berlin, alone, and on foot, a fugitive heroine, in difguife, no doubt, with a bundle in your hand, and a large ftraw hat tied under your chin, beneath which fhould be difcovered a certain dignified and noble air, which fome piteous ftage-coachman perceiving fhould give you a place on the box. This, no doubt, would be vaftly clever and in- terefting, but the way I mean to propofe is much lefs dangerous and more fimple. One of my former maids is married to the poft-mafter of the city. She is entirely de- voted to me, and her hufband will not only furnifh a chaife and horfes but conduct you himfelf; will accompany you till you get fafe to your brother, and, if you pleafe, you may now efcape, and wait at their houfe till you fet off. You have your choice to do

this

this or marry de Zaftrow; for there is no alternative; you muft determine for the marriage or the elopement; and, if you let the moment flip, it will be impoffible for me to ferve you."

"My choice is made," faid I, inftantly; "and, fure, I am moft fortunate in a friend. I will fly to my brother, who will protect me for my Lindorf——And yet it is a great crime to deceive my aunt."

"Your aunt thinks it none to deceive you, moft unworthily."

"But fuppofe I were to try, once more, to move her."——

"Your trial would be vain. Tears, prayers, perfecutions, and even faintings, are

are expected, which, far from being moved at, they perhaps will profit by."

" I will be gone," cried I; " neither fcruples nor remorfe fhall ftay me. I am fhamefully treated, and I have no longer any other inquietude than that which the fear of efcaping in fafety gives."

" Nothing is eafier. Take my gown, cloak, and veil; they will fuppofe it me, and leave me to follow you. Wait for me at our houfe, I will prefently be with you."

" Mademoifelle de Manteul is not very fcrupulous," faid the Count, fmiling. " You cannot imagine half her zeal," continued Matilda. I myfelf was incapable of either acting or thinking; but fhe, in a moment, got every thing ready, helped me

to

to put on my difguife, opened the door, kiffed me, pufhed me forwards, and faid, "Go, go, dear Matilda; you have not a moment to lofe: they may be coming here the next minute, perhaps; fly, or farewell all hope." Fear gave me courage, and I had got to the bottom of the ftaircafe when I recollected I ought to write a note, and leave it on my table, for my aunt; that fhe might be certain, at leaft, I was not dead. I returned, and Mademoifelle de Manteul, terrified at feeing me, thought I had met fome one on the ftairs. Scarcely had I begun to tell her what brought me back before fhe interrupted me. "You are mad," faid fhe; "Write a letter! Give your aunt time to come and catch you! She told me fhe was coming up prefently——Begone, begone! They are

not

not fo eafily to be perfuaded people are going to kill themfelves as you are !"

" The fear of being caught made me compliant, and I got out without being perceived. I had not far to go, nor was it long before my friend came to me. " We have a whole hour to take our meafures in," faid fhe; " they think you are afleep, and I advifed them to leave you in peace, at prefent. The firft thing you have to do, therefore, is to go to the poft-houfe; for, fhould they find you abfent, they will come to feek you here immediately. You will there remain in fafety. If you want any money I can affift you."

" Thanks to your goodnefs, my brother, I did not want this kind of affiftance. My friend, therefore, went with me to the miftrefs

trefs of the poft-houfe, who confented to
every thing fhe propofed, and with whom
fhe left me. It was very probable they
would come to feek me at the houfe of
Mademoifelle de Manteul, and, therefore,
neceffary fhe fhould be at home to avoid
fufpicion.

" No fooner was I alone than I began to
be deeply affected at the terror of my aunt,
when fhe found me gone, and was wholly
ignorant what was become of me. Dif-
obedience and flight were fufficient of-
fences, and needed not aggravation. I,
therefore, refolved to repair them, as far as
was in my power, and, having called for
pen, ink, and paper, wrote nearly thus. :

" I have juft been informed, my dear
" aunt, my brother is at Berlin, and am
" fo

" fo impatient to fee him that I have gone
" without afking a permiffion which, in
" all probability, would have been refufed,
" and have thus fpared myfelf the regret
" of a denial and again being difobedient.
" I am already fufficiently afflicted for
" having difpleafed you by my refiftance
" to your will. Ah! why, my dear aunt,
" have you forced me thus to difpleafe,
" thus to refufe compliance, thus to fly
" from you? How happy fhould I have
" been could I have contributed to your
" felicity! The Baron de Zaftrow muft
" have fufficient delicacy to feel that a pro-
" mife, extorted by terror and difowned by
" the heart, is not binding. I hope he
" will no more think of killing himfelf,
" for I am no longer there to catch his
" arm; I would earneftly advife him to
" live

" live, and, and, above all, to live happy with-
" out Matilda."

" I gave this note in charge to one of the
landlady's children, and bade him deliver
it to the porter, without saying who it came
from. More at eafe, now I thought my
aunt would be fo too, I waited with tolerable patience for Mademoifelle de Manteul, who had promifed to fee me again
before I fet off, and who, at length, came.

" You have not a moment to lofe,"
faid fhe ; " you muft depart at day-break ;
the Baron is fearching you through every
houfe in town; he has juft left ours, and
I encouraged him to continue this fearch,
which will give you time to get the ftart.
It was exceedingly lucky you did not write,
as your filly whim would have made you."—
I durft

I durft not confefs I juft had wrote, but I now felt my imprudence, and the fear of being purfued was fo ftrong that I was un-, willing to go. My friend employed all her eloquence to encourage me; fhe defcribed the anger of my aunt, the neceffity I fhould be under of confeffing where I had been, and who. had affifted me, the afcendant which my elopement and return would give her over me; told me there would be no poffibility of appeafing but by obeying her, and that, if ever I entered her houfe again, fhe was certain I fhould be married within two hours.—"I will go," faid I; "I will go inftantly; the die is caft, and, be the event what it will, I will go;" and accordingly orders to get the chaife and horfes ready were immediately given. Mademoifelle de Manteul, fearing I again fhould relapfe, would not leave me. She was

under

under no apprehensions about her father,
whose gout kept him at home; she sent
him word that she should sup out, and remained with me till the moment of departure. Of de Zaftrow, of my brother, of
Lindorf, of every thing that might encourage me to keep my resolution, she spoke.
"Depend on me," said she; "I will go, in
the morning, to de Zaftrow, and lead him
to suspect you are flown to England. He
shall not easily get away from me, and by
that time you will be so far on the way to
Berlin that all pursuit will be in vain." This
gave me a little confidence; or, rather,
it was now too late to listen to fear. To recede was no longer possible, and I beheld
the moment of departure arrive with pleasure. Unable to express my gratitude,
except by my kisses and tears, while my
friend was enraptured to see me, as she
said,

said, escape so many dangers, I got into the chaise and"——

" Alone !" interrupted the Count.

" No; the mistress of the house, who is now with me, and who, formerly, as I said, had served Mademoiselle de Manteul, whose husband conducted us"——

" But where is Lindorf?" replied the Count, again stopping her short. " It seems that Mademoiselle de Manteul, not he, has carried you off."

" And did you think it was Lindorf?"

" I own, I am glad to find it was not; though there seems something incomprehensible in all this!

" A little

" A little patience, brother, and you
will not hereafter judge of your Matilda
from appearances.

" And now, behold me in the poſt-chaiſe,
with the good Marianne, for that is her
name; eſcorted by her huſband, on horſe-
back, ſtopping only to change horſes,
toſſing ducats into the poſtillion's hats, and
taking each buſh for the Baron de Zaſtrow.
My companion did all ſhe could to inſpire
courage. Mademoiſelle de Manteul was
her oracle, and ſhe, every minute, repeated
" there was nothing to fear, for Mademoiſelle had told her ſo." Theſe aſſurances
made me more tranquil; and, having travelled the firſt day without interruption, I
thought myſelf in perfect ſafety. Juſt,
however, as we came yeſterday to the poſt-
houſe, I, very imprudently, put my head

VOL. III.　　　K　　　out

out of the carriage, and, prefently, heard a voice, I thought I knew, cry, "It is fhe! It is fhe herfelf! Poftillion! Stop! On your life ftop!" And I prefently faw young de Zaftrow, at the fide of the chaife, with a thoufand menaces in his countenance."

"De Zaftrow!" cried the Count and Caroline.

"Yes; De Zaftrow, and without the help of witchcraft. What, you fuppofe fome malicious fairy has winged him through the air. Nay, to fay the truth, I fuppofed fo myfelf, at firft; but, alas! I foon found this good for nothing fairy was neither more nor lefs than my own imprudence. The note I had written had indicated the road I fhould take, and the Ba-

ron had not loft his time in further fearch
at Drefden. He fuppofed I had, no doubt,
written it, in the carriage, and, that, by
fetting off immediately, he fhould eafily
overtake and bring me back; and this fuppofition made him depart two or three
hours before me. I imagined myfelf purfued, while, on the contrary, I was full fpeed
purfuing, and, unfortunately enough, over-
took him at this poft-houfe, where he was
waiting for horfes. How great muft have
been the furprife of my dear friend, Mademoifelle de Manteul, when fhe found, in
the morning, he was gone! And how exceffive her inquietude and fears for me!
At prefent, however, I hope fhe is eafier."

"Yes, yes," faid the Count, fmiling,
"fhe is eafy enough, never fear. But go
on with your ftory, it is quite romantic."

"Ro-

"Romantic, indeed! I assure you, I think it a very extraordinary story! But we are not half at the end of it yet—Let me see—Terror, fright, and consternation, at the sight of de Zaltrow. Yes, yes; I was there—Well, then: I shrieked, and hid myself in a corner of the chaise, while Marianne screamed to the postillion to go on; de Zaltrow threatened and bade him stop, his servants came up, and the crowd increased. Something must be done, and I thought it best to speak to the Baron, to ask him by what right he interrupted me, or pretended to deprive me of my liberty, and to tell him, openly, I would rather die than either marry him or return to Dresden. Accordingly I again looked out of the chaise, and there I saw!—

"Now, if you please, you may talk of witchcraft,

witchcraft, fairies, and romances; any
thing, or every thing, you can suppofe mi-
-raculous and inconceivable; for there did
I fee—Lindorf! Yes, Lindorf himfelf;
who, inftead of in England, was there,
befide the chaife, as much aftonifhed as
myfelf. Matilda!—Lindorf!—Thefe exclamations were mutual and inftantaneous,
and I really believed heaven had fent him
to my fuccour; therefore, leaping out of
the chaife—

"I cannot go on," faid Matilda, "you
muft finifh the ftory, Lindorf; you know
the remainder better than I do." Then,
with her head reclined on the fhoulder of
Caroline, fhe whifpered, "I hope he will
not tell how I fprang into his arms and
clafped him in mine with all my ftrength."

" Aye,

" Aye, aye, let me conjure thee, dear Lindorf, to go on," said the Count, impatiently; " prithée, explain by what ſtrange chance thou cameſt, juſt at that preciſe moment, on the Dreſden road, and in company with the Baron de Zaſtrow."

" I had returned," ſaid Lindorf, " to anſwer, in perſon, the charming, the tender letter I had received at London. My being there at this moment was accidental, but I was not in company with the Baron de Zaſtrow. It was chance, or, rather, my guardian genius that brought me to the poſt-houſe juſt then. I was unacquainted with the Baron, but I ſaw a young man of quality, impatient to obtain horſes, and quite furious becauſe none were to be found. He inquired, at the ſame time, if a young lady, whom he endea-

endeavoured to deſcribe, had not lately
paſſed that road. They anſwered, no, and
he again, began to ſwear it was falſe, ſhe
muſt have paſſed; and again to beſtow
his curſes on the poſtillions and the poſt-
maſter. As ſoon as I alighted from my
chaiſe, for I was going to Dreſden, he
came up, and ſaid, " you, certainly, Sir,
muſt have met a young lady, alone, very
handſome, driving full ſpeed!"

" No, Sir, I aſſure you, I met no ſuch
lady; nor, indeed, any lady, that I remember."

" This is very extraordinary!" ſaid he,
ſtamping—" Perhaps the note was a new
trick!—Excuſe me, Sir, for queſtioning you
ſo abruptly. I am purſuing a woman I
adore, who promiſed me her hand yeſterday,

was

was to have married me to-day, and who eloped laſt night!"

"The misfortune is the greater," anſwered I, "Sir, becauſe you do not ſeem that kind of perſon the ladies would fly." My compliment ſeemed to pleaſe him, and acquired me his entire confidence. He bowed, and, with much ſelf-ſufficiency, which he endeavoured to render modeſt, replied, "I own, Sir, it is not the firſt time I have been told ſo; and there have been ladies who have gone farther than telling; but you ſee how different taſtes are; and, certainly, that of women is very often very capricious. Is it not quite extraordinary that her I am purſuing is yet not eighteen; and that, notwithſtanding, ſhe has a whim of romantic fidelity for a lover who has forſaken her, and whom
ſhe

fhe will never fee again? I am unacquainted with him, but fhould fuppofe perfonal
accomplifhments not *infinitely* in his favour; and, as to birth and fortune, in thefe
I yield to no man."

" All this, Sir, I make no doubt, is
true; but if your rival has the advantage
of being beloved"—

" Beloved, or not beloved," faid he, " it
is equal to me; he is abfent, will fee her
no more; if I can overtake her, fhe is
mine, and fhall be obliged to adore me."

" This converfation paffed before the poft-
houfe, and I was amazed at the facility with
which this indifcreet and vain young man
fpoke to a ftranger, as well as at his total
want of delicacy, and filently approved the

fugitive

fugitive lady. Juft then a chaife came up,
full gallop, from Drefden, and interrupted
us. He did not feem to have the leaft
fufpicion, and looked towards it from mere
curiofity, till, the chaife ftopping, a lady
looked out. I had but a glimpfe, and did
not know it was Matilda, but my gentleman, inftantly, exclaimed, " It is fhe!
It is fhe!" While the lady drew back, ex-
claiming, in her turn, " It is he!" The
maid bade the poftillion drive on, while de
Zaftrow, with uplifted cane, threatened to
knock him off his horfe if he moved a
ftep. I hefitated, for a moment, what part
I fhould take. The franknefs of the youth
had, in fome meafure, laid me under an
obligation; and yet I felt myfelf affected
for the unfortunate lady, whom they were
going to marry againft her confent. My
firft intention was to become a mediator,

if

if poffible, and to infpire the terrified lady
with fortitude, for which purpofe I approached the chaife, far from imagining
how deeply I myfelf was interefted in this
adventure. As I came up I heard my
own name repeated in an accent of amaze-
ment! The door opened, and out flew
Matilda, whom I inftantly knew, notwithftanding the finifhed beauty, alteration, and growth, of her perfon! The
charming Matilda placed herfelf by my
fide, took me by the hand, and faid, in a
voice which terror and joy had rendered
faint, " Dear, dear Lindorf! God has
furely fent you to the affiftance and de-
fence of your Matilda! They want to
rob you of her, but they never never
fhall! She will be yours, and yours only."

" No fooner did the Baron hear my

name

-name than, throwing away his cane, draw-ing his fword, and arrogantly advancing, he exclaimed, " Lindorf! What treachery is this?" Then, addreffing himfelf to Matilda, faid, " I entreat, Mademoifelle, you will go into my poft-chaife. I have the pofitive commands of your aunt to bring you back to Drefden, and I dare fay the Baron of Lindorf will not think proper to oppofe thofe commands."

" That we fhall prefently fee, Sir," anfwered, I coldly, while I fupported Matilda, whom fo many contending paffions had occafioned to faint in my arms. I gently carried her into the poft-houfe and laid her on the firft bed I found; then, recommending her to the perfons prefent, telling them they fhould be anfwerable for her forthcoming, I immediately left her, and went in fearch of the Baron de Zaftrow. I
found

found him demanding entrance, and forcia
bly withheld by two or three men, who
let him go the moment I appeared. We
walked together to fome diftance, and
went into an enclofed garden. "You have
accufed me of treachery, fir," faid I, "and
appearances may give fome fmall juftification to the fufpicion; but I affure you,
on my honour, that chance, only, a moft
lucky one it is true, has brought me here.
When I fpoke to you, I was ignorant both
that you were my rival, and that Matilda had fled. If you think this fufficient
fatisfaction, and will leave the young Countefs of Walftein abfolute miftrefs of herfelf,
I promife you to abide by her decifion, and
here offer you my future friendfhip and
efteem; if not, I will defend my own pretenfions and her liberty at the hazard of
my life."

"Defend

"Defend them, then, traitor," replied he, attacking me with fo much impetuofity that, being off my guard, I received a wound in the left arm. It was not danger-ous, and only roufed my anger; and the Baron took fo little care, thinking himfelf certain of victory, when he faw me wound-ed, that I eafily difarmed him. His fword flew out of his hand and, as it fell, I fet my foot on it—"Your life," faid I, "is now in my power; I am wounded and you are not; but, difregarding this fmall difad-vantage, I am ready to reftore your fword, and, again, put it to the chance of victory, if you do not renounce your pretenfions to Matilda, and promife to depart for Drefden, immediately, without feeing her."

"He hefitated, and I faw, by the change of his countenance, my manner of acting.

had

had made fome impreffion. Pride ftill
ftruggled, but honour, at laft, was con-
queror, and he prefented his hand. " Re-
" collect," faid he, " Sir, you have, on
thefe conditions, offered your efteem and
friendfhip. I feel, at prefent, I fhall be
proud of and will, therefore, endeavour to
merit them, by prevailing on my aunt to
confirm that happinefs which is juftly your
due. Forget the paft, and make my peace
with Matilda. I pretend only to her
friendfhip; though," added he, with a
mixture of former felf-fufficiency; " I am
not accuftomed to difdain; nor do I know
by what fafcination I fo long have fupported hers." I embraced him, faid fhe
would certainly be the laft cruel beauty he
would find, and that, had not her heart
been pre-engaged fhe could not poffibly
have

have refifted fo many accomplifhments and
fo much merit; after which we parted the
beft friends in the world.

" As foon as I faw him get into his
chaife, I haftened to Matilda, concerning
whom I was very uneafy. Her fainting,
however, was moft happily timed, fince it
deprived her of the knowledge of a tranfaction that might have occafioned dreadful
terrors. She began to recover and, looking round her, afked where fhe was, as I
entered; then, refuming all her accuftomed grace, " Dear Lindorf," faid fhe, " and
is it not a dream? Is it true that I have
once more found thee, and that we never
fhall forfake each other again ?"

Scarcely had Lindorf finifhed his
phrafe ere he felt the white hand of Matilda

tilda upon his mouth.—" Fie, fie, young
gentleman," faid fhe, " I fee no occafion
to repeat all that paffed fo literally. My
dear brother, and my dear, dear fifter, do
not believe a word he fays. For, what if
I had thought all that, can you fuppofe
I would have fpoken my thoughts? And,
even, if I did, you know I was fainting.
Who can tell what they do after fo ftrange
a meeting, preffed by one lover, protected
by another, and amongft rencounters and
battles, and all this hurly burly? One may
be allowed to be a little extravagant and
filly, on fuch occafions; but, at prefent,
I affure you, I am as prudent as"—Matilda
fmiled, with malicious pleafure, on Lindorf; then, fuddenly clafping his hand,
added, " Well then, I fay again and again,
every thing I faid yefterday! And I hope
we fhall never forfake each other more!"

Matilda

Matilda was fo charming, as fhe faid this, and there was fuch a mixture of rapture, pleafantry, and confufion in her countenance, that Lindorf imagined he loved her dearer than ever he had loved woman, and expreffed himfelf with fo much enthufiafm and fire that every body thought the fame. Caroline was tranfported, fhe kiffed the Count, and faid, " Was I wrong when I told you how dearly he would love her?" Walftein beheld Lindorf with aftonifhment, nor yet could comprehend, perfectly, all he heard and faw. To reafon and friendfhip he had attributed the attachment of Lindorf to Matilda; for well he recollected to what excefs he had adored Caroline; nor could imagine how a paffion fo energetic might fo foon change its object. Yet was there every appearance of fincerity in his manner, and

words;

words; and Lindorf was no hypocrite.
Beside, the Count was so accustomed to
read his thoughts that, had he been
under any real constraint, it could not have
escaped him, and he could observe nothing
but sincerity. Lindorf, on his part,
guessed what was passing in the mind of
the Count, and whispered, "when we are
alone, dear Walstein, you shall hear my
story, and your surprise will then not be so
great. In the mean time, do not imagine
your friend has acquired a facility at feign-
ing; or that he does not feel all he ex-
presses." The Count clasped his hand,
and entreated Matilda to finish her story.
There was not much to say, but the least
circumstance was interesting to the Count
and Caroline. Matilda replied, "You forget, brother, that Lindorf is the historian,
at present."—Lindorf thus continued.

"I found

" I found a village furgeon to drefs my
wound, and hoped I might have concealed
it from Matilda, as well as my conteft
with the Baron. I, therefore, only told
her he had liftened to reafon, departed for
Drefden, and promifed to appeafe his aunt.
She was moft happy at the intelligence,
and, being equally impatient to fee our
friend and brother, we prefently departed.
The motion of the carriage, and, perhaps,
the emotion of my heart, foon difturbed
my wound, and Matilda was greatly agitated when fhe faw the blood. It was impoffible any longer to conceal the caufe,
and we were obliged to ftop here to drefs
it again. It was found deeper than had
been imagined, and I was condemned to
take four and twenty hours repofe. In
vain did I folicit my lovely partner to
continue her journey, and leave me in this
wretched

wretched inn; no entreaties could gain her confent."

"No, to be fure," interrupted Matilda, with vivacity. "I know my duty better. Who ever heard of a heroine of romance abandoning her wounded knight, who had defended her againft a ferocious ravifher? I even thought it neceffary, according to cuftom, to drefs that wound myfelf, and bathe it with my tears. Did not I, Lindorf? And I hope you will own I tied the fcarf with tolerable grace. Was not my attitude and manner affecting, brother?"

"The very picture of a princefs of the age of Amadis."

"No; one of the miftreffes of the famous Galaor," faid fhe, glancing at Lindorf.

"It

"It was the miftrefs, then, that fixed the rover," replied he, kiffing her hand.

"So faid Galaor to every miftrefs, and they believed him; but I," continued Matilda, "am not fo credulous, and mean to put your fincerity to the proof—In thofe times, a woman, with vaft *fang froid,* commanded her lover not to pronounce a fingle word for two years, and he obeyed. Oh! happy age! I, though I only fhall impofe reft and filence on my wounded hero till to-morrow, am certain to find him difobedient!"

"Never, never," faid Lindorf kneeling; "and there will be fome merit in my fubmiffion, for I have many things to tell my Walftein."

"And fo you would have paffed a whole night

night in chattering; mean while the fever
and the wound?—I reiterate my abfolute
command!—Silence and reft till to-morrow !"

Exact obedience was promifed, though
not without reluctance. The friends were
both impatient to communicate their fentiments; and, particularly, the Count, who
was doubly interefted to find the heart of
Lindorf cured of paffion for Caroline, and
capable of making Matilda happy. It was,
therefore, agreed that, in recompenfe for
this their filence, they fhould travel, on
the morrow, in the chaife of Lindorf, and
leave the coach of the Count to the ladies.
This arrangement was equally acceptable
to Caroline, who was herfelf moft defirous
the friends fhould mutually explain their
feelings, that Walftein might be convinced

of

of the exact truth of all fhe had told him, and inform Lindorf of her prefent love for her hufband. Matilda, perhaps, might have preferred the care of her wounded knight; but Matilda dared not fay fo; and her brother having mentioned fending his fervant to Drefden, with letters for his aunt, fhe-alfo retired to write, both to her and Mademoifelle de Manteul, to whom fhe fent back the fervants and chaife.

She prefently returned with her two letters. The Count read that to Madam de Zaftrow, approved it, added a few lines from himfelf, and, perceiving Matilda concealed the one fhe had written to Mademoifelle de Manteul, faid, fmiling, " I fuppofe you exprefs your gratitude in ftrong terms to your zealous friend."

" I ex-

" I exprefs it as I feel it; and, I think, that is faying a great deal. You, who are one of the heroes of friendfhip, ought, certainly, to be delighted to find fuch an inftance of its effects; efpecially in a woman."——The Count continued to fmile.——" And pray now, what is the meaning of that ironic air? What, you are incredulous?—Sifter Caroline, I hope you will take the part of the fex."

" We will both take its part," anfwered Caroline, " and prove how capable women are of friendfhip."

" I never doubted it," replied Walftein; " nay, I even believe that pure difinter- efted friendfhip is lefs rare among women than it is fuppofed. It is a fenfation wholly accordant to their gentle and tender nature;

but you will forgive me for not imagining Mademoifelle de Manteul one of its models."

" Brother!—After fo many proofs!"

" I am almoft forry, dear Matilda, to rob you of that happy credulity which fo well proves the innocence of your heart; but, I muft own, I have very ftrong doubts concerning thofe proofs. Mademoifelle de Manteul appeared greatly affected; but was it for you or for herfelf? Was it to ferve a friend or to get rid of a rival? Every circumftance, I think, befpeaks the latter."

Matilda was confounded. A thoufand little incidents were recollected, and a thoufand others rufhed forward to prove her brother was right; yet could fhe not instantly inftantly give her up, and replied, with vivacity; "Surely you muft be deceived, fhe diflikes, nay, detefts the Baron; fhe was always fpeaking ill of and turning him to ridicule."

"Right, right; to augment your repugnance. This is the very caufe why I fay fhe is not a true friend. Had Mademoifelle de Manteul, the victim of an involuntary paffion, opened her heart to you, and given you fecret for fecret; had you together concerted the means of avoiding a marriage that muft render you both unhappy, I fhould have faith in her friendfhip, and even be far from blaming her; but all this artifice at her age is odious: fhe only had herfelf in view by prompting you to an imprudent ftep, which the event has juftified, but which might have been your deftruction."

L 2

Lindorf,

Lindorf, here, took up the subject. "You are too severe, dear Walstein; be the motives of Mademoiselle de Manteul what they may, she has served me so essentially that it becomes me to undertake her justification, and I see nothing in all this but artifice which may well be permitted to love; besides, while she was serving herself, she was, also, saving her friend from inevitable misfortune."

"No doubt," said Matilda, who took courage at seeing herself supported; "for one day longer, and I had been forced to marry that odious Baron."

"And do you not perceive, my dear girl, that, I being on the road, one day longer and you had been for ever freed from tyranny, without that violence which is ever prejudicial

prejudicial to a young lady's reputation, and without offence to an aunt to whose cares you are certainly much indebted? Your only error, dear Matilda, was that of suspecting my friendship; of supposing, for an instant, I could abandon you; and of blindly confiding in an imprudent young lady, though, I own, she is rather to blame than you."

"Dear, dear brother," cried Matilda, all in tears, and running into his arms, "pardon us both. Ah! how do I reproach myself for having mentioned, for having given you an ill opinion of her! But so far was I from suspecting it that I supposed you would admire her conduct and her zeal."

Lindorf joined Matilda, and chid his friend for his severity. Caroline clasped

her

her to her bofom, and, while fhe wiped away her tears, wept in concert——" Think not I wifh ill to Mademoifelle de Manteul," faid the Count, exceedingly affected. " No, to her I owe the happinefs of beholding thofe I love united. So freely do I pardon her that I fincerely hope fhe may marry de Zaftrow, and will even fpeak in her behalf to my aunt. And now, Matilda, do thou pardon me for having afflicted and undeceived thee. It will be a leffon to thee, my dear, and the laft I fhall ever give thee; for, from this moment, I commit thy conduct, and thy felicity to Lindorf. Thou knoweft how ardently I have defired to fee thee his. Oh! Caroline, Oh! my fifter, Oh! my friend, fcarcely can my heart contain its joys, the fweet fenfations this happy moment brings!"

Matilda

Matilda a thoufand times thanked her brother for his fincerity, and for the inftruction it contained. "Though," faid fhe, "I fcarcely can repent my imprudence, fince it has made us all happy a day fooner." And added that fhe would, in a poftfcript, let Mademoifelle de Manteul pleafantly underftand that, at prefent, fhe was acquainted with her motives.——The Count was not at all deceived in his conjectures, for Mademoifelle de Manteul had been folely prompted by her paffion for the young Baron de Zaftrow, who had paid her fome attentions before he went on his travels, and who, fhe hoped, would have married her on his return. The arrival of Matilda at Drefden, the wifhes of her aunt, the attachment of the young Baron to the amiable fpoufe deftined him, all repelled hopes which Matilda's love of Lindorf once more

animated.

animated. She had only fought her friendfhip to have an opportunity of feeing the
Baron revive his former fentiments, difcover thofe of Matilda, and, if poffible,
turn them towards fome other object. At
firft fhe had had her brother in view, and,
therefore, had fhewn Matilda his letter;
but her joy was exceffive when fhe learned
this lover already exifted, and that her
young rival was determined on the moft
peremptory refiftance. This it was her
advantage to encourage all in her power;
but this alone was not fufficient; the beft
means of obtaining her own end, fhe fuppofed, would be to remove Matilda from
Drefden. This might beft be done by
engaging her to take fome ftep which
fhould abfolutely break off the intended
match. She it was who perfuaded Madam
de Zaftrow, and her nephew, that, by ter-
rifying

rifying Matilda, they might obtain her
consent; and what the consequence of this
terror and the succefs of her schemes were
has already been seen. Yet was she but
little benefited by her artifice, for the
young Baron, recognizing, in the post-
chaise, the former maid of Mademoiselle
de Manteul, and being convinced she had
favored Matilda's flight, was irritated at the
perfidious trick that had been played him.
But this perfidy was the consequence of
affection; and when the vanity of man is
flattered he is generally indulgent.

Return we to our happy travellers. The
wound of Lindorf healed apace, so excellent a balsamic is happinefs, and they set
off for Berlin; Caroline and Matilda in
one of the carriages, and the two friends in
the other. Leave we these lovely ladies to

speak

ſpeak of thoſe they held moſt dear, to con-
gratulate each other, to form plans of future delight, and to vow eternal friendſhip. Leave we them frequently to look
out of the carriage after the poſt-chaiſe that
followed, wiſhing impatiently to arrive,
and let us examine how Walſtein and Lindorf paſſed their time.

They partook of the impatience we have
mentioned; but man feels not ſo ſenſibly
thoſe ſhort privations which are ſubjects of
ſuch real uneaſineſs to the tender heart of
woman. Perhaps, on great occaſions, the
former may be more ardent, more paſſionate, more capable of riſking every thing
for the object of their love; but the daily
proofs, the intervening fears, and all the
ſhades of a delicate and conſtant paſſion,
are much more peculiar to women; few
men

men are fufceptible of them, nay, few know
their value. Our travellers, indeed, had
not time to think of them; yet had they
been in the chaife fome time without entering into any converfation. They fat
filent, for Lindorf knew not where to begin,
or what to fay to the hufband of Caroline,
and the Count feared left the moft trifling
queftion might bear the afpect of reproach:
he, however, was the firft to fpeak, and
told his friend how much he had been
afflicted by reading the manufcript he had
left with Caroline. " I have not the leaft
fear or fcruple," faid he, " in confiding the
happinefs of a fifter to the man to whom I
am fo infinitely indebted, and who, loving
and beloved by the moft angelic woman
the world contains, could not only facrifice
his own paffion, but endeavour to infpire
her with love for another. Ah! dear

Lindorf," faid.he, " while to you I owe the heart of Caroline and the felicity of Matilda, is it poffible Lever can acquit myfelf of the wondrous debt? Yet, fpeak, explain how this fudden revolution in your affections, which yet I underftand not, has happened. Is not all you teftify for my fifter another facrifice of generous friend-fhip? Endeavour not to impofe upon yourfelf. Can Caroline——

" Dear Walftein," interrupted Lindorf, inftantly, "I would utter oaths if I did not know the word of your friend were fuf-ficient. Believe that friend, then, when he affures you he is worthy of becoming your brother; and that nothing has he ex-preffed that he has not felt. I love Caro-line, no doubt, but it is as I love her huf-band, with friendfhip as pure and ftrong as

it

it is durable; but I love my dear Matilda as the fole woman on earth who now can make me happy—You are furprifed, but hear what I have to fay. Learn what has paffed in the heart you yourfelf have formed fince laft we parted."

The Count was moft defirous to hear, and fat attentive while Lindorf thus continued.

" Since you have read my manufcript, Walftein, you are informed of my firft acquaintance with Caroline, and what were the fentiments fhe infpired. I fhall attempt no juftification of myfelf. You can judge whether it be poffible to fee her with indifference. I proteft, however, before heaven, that, notwithftanding all her beauty, all her charms, fhe would have been

totally

totally indifferent to me had I had the leaſt
ſuſpicion ſhe was your wife. But this how
might I have? You were ſilent; Caroline,
then ſo young, bore not your name, and
the good Canoneſs gave evident marks of
wiſhing to ſee us united. Every circumſtance told me ſhe was free and that I might
dare to love her———Oh! wherefore, my
friend, that fatal reſerve?———Yet let us
paſs this over. Ignorant in my guilt, I
offended the man for whom I would willingly have ſacrificed my life; he has ſeen
ſome faint picture of my grief, my remorſe,
and the reſolution I took, the inſtant I diſ-
covered my crime, to fly. I thought I
might, in ſome meaſure, repair the involuntary wrong I had done by ſhewing Caroline who and what the huſband was ſhe
fled. I knew her ſoul congenial to yours,
capable of eſtimating its worth, and that

you

you were formed to admire and adore each other."

" It was thy noble friendſhip," exclaimed the Count, " which alone could draw me with ſuch features and ſuch colours as could affeĉt the heart of Caroline. Yes, dear Lindorf, to thee alone I owe that heart and all the exquiſite felicity I enjoy. No, had it not been for that paſſion with which thou ſo continually reproacheſt thyſelf, Caroline, perhaps, never had loved me. But go on, dear friend, I long to be convinced thou art equally happy, and that thou thinkeſt Matilda a proper recompenſe for the ſublime efforts thou haſt made to conquer a paſſion which could diĉtate the manuſcript thou lefteſt at Rindaw and baniſh thee from Caroline."

" I left

"I left her," replied Lindorf, " determined never to see her more, till, by wholly subduing my fatal passion, I were worthy her and you; and far was I from foreseeing this blifsful moment was so near. The solitude of Ronebourg augmented my love and gloomy melancholy; inceffantly did fancy tranfport me to the pavilion of Rindaw, inceffantly was Caroline prefent. I faw her, heard her, converfed with her, and when the fweet illufion vanifhed, defpair and remorfe acquired additional ftrength, and they were tried to the utmoft by your arrival and converfation. You loved Caroline, your happinefs depended on being beloved by her, and again I renewed my vow of furmounting my paffion; or, rather, of forfaking my country, and carefully concealing from you I had been your rival. This

vow

vow had been held facred; never had the
name of Caroline efcaped my lips had not
fhe, like an apparition, appeared at Ronebourg, the occafion of which I yet underftand not, and deprived me of reafon.
Excufe me from defcribing all I felt while
I thought I beheld her dying, but imagine what it muft be when it could make
me betray the fecret of my heart, and inform you that a friend, towards whom
you had acted with fuch magnanimity, was
the guilty lover of your wife!

    " My determination was to take ven-
geance on myfelf, and follow her whom I
thought dead; but figns of returning life
prevented me: fhe was reftored to you,
and I wifhed not to interrupt your happinefs by the horrid fpectacle of fuicide. I
went into my room, wrote the letter you
found,

found, mounted my horfe, and rode full
fpeed, without knowing whither I went,
or having fo much as a fingle fervant with
me. The firft day I fuffered my horfe to
take which road he pleafed, and, at night,
ftopped at a wretched inn ; I endeavoured,
however, to collect my ideas, and refolved
to follow my firft intention, which was
to go to England. I had written to court
and obtained permiffion for that purpofe, my fervant and baggage might foon
follow, and I immediately took the road
to Hamburg, where I meant to embark.
I rode poft day and night, and this continual change of fcene correfponded with
the agitation of my foul, to which repofe
was infupportable. I wifhed to find a
veffel ready to fail to Hamburg, and to
ftep into it as I got out of my chaife ; but,
happily, there were none ready. Some

hours

hours after my arrival, I was feized with
a burning fever, which lafted feveral days;
the phyfician, whom my hoft called in,
had me bled fo abundantly that exceffive
weaknefs was the confequence, and retard-
ed my departure. Obliged to remain at
Hamburg till I gathered ftrength, I wrote
to my valet de chambre to come to me
there. My ficknefs was the natural confequence of my feelings, and the fatigues
of my journey, and was certainly a fortunate one. It calmed the violence of my
tranfports, and obliged me to follow the
plan I myfelf had laid down, as foon as I
knew you to be the hufband of Caroline.

"At prefent, when I no longer feel this
weaknefs, I may own that more than twenty
times on the road was I tempted to return to Ronebourg, and from your hand
demand

demand Caroline or death. Had I been obliged to remain at Hamburg, without falling ill, perhaps, I fhould have been overcome, and for ever have rendered my-felf unworthy your efteem and friendfhip. My fever, and its confequent weaknefs, fhewed me objects under a different point of view; and, whether the organization of the body influences the mind, whether it was the refult of reflections inceffantly made, or whether friendfhip really triumphed over love, certain it is my paffion, each day, became feebler; or rather, reafon became ftronger. I ftill adored Caroline, but I adored her as a deity, without daring to fuppofe I again might fee her. I fhud-dered even at the idea, and, far from wifhing to return, I wifhed to remove far-ther off, and therefore waited impatiently for Varner.

" Such

" Such was the temper of my mind when
the young Baron de Manteul arrived at
Hamburg, and came to lodge in the same
hotel; my hoft immediately informed him
of my illnefs, exaggerated the danger I
had been in, the care he had taken of me,
the flow recovery of my ftrength, and infpired him with a wifh to become acquainted with me. He fent up his com-
pliments, and, as his was a Saxon family
well known, I received him with pleafure.
His appearance gave me a favourable impreffion, which was confirmed by his converfation. He was equally pleafed with
me, and in a few hours we were old friends.
He, likewife, was going to England, but
could not ftop more than three days at
Hamburg: hearing I intended to crofs the
fea, he earneftly entreated me to embark on
board the fame fhip. My health, which

daily

daily grew ftronger, permitted me to depart, and I willingly confented to a requeft
by which I fhould gain fuch an agreeable
companion. I left a letter of inftructions
for my valet with the hoft, and in two
days we left Hamburg, mutually congra-
tulating each other on this lucky rencontre :
we further agreed to live together, at London, and take lodgings in the fame houfe.

" This young gentleman was the more
agreeable to me for being almoft as melancholy as myfelf, and we often fighed in
fympathy: he firft made the remark.
During the voyage we were alone on the
deck, each abforbed in his own ideas, and
each preferving the moft profound filence.
Manteul at length fpoke; " I think," faid
he, " I have difcovered another conformity
between us. Is it not true, dear Lindorf,

4   that

that your heart is engaged, and that you deeply regret some person whom you have left in your own country?" I, not choosing to give a direct answer, retorted the question, and told him he had made the confession."

" I own it," replied he; " and, did you know the person I regret, you, then, would have some knowledge of what my feelings are. When I quitted Saxony, I imagined I fled from the danger of loving the most charming woman in the world; but, now I see her no more, I feel the mischief is done, and that I fled too late."

" I owned my heart was as much enslaved as his; but added nothing farther; I rather endeavoured to turn the conversation, by making reflections on the pangs and effects of love.—

" We

" We had a good voyage and arrived
fafe at London. The novelty of this vaft
city, its riches, the multitude of its inhabitants, and that peculiarity of manners
which diftance and a government fo different produce, greatly relieved my melancholy; and, as I moft fincerely defired to
be wholly cured of it, I myfelf ardently
fought amufement. I recovered health and
ftrength apace, and even a part of my natural cheerfulnefs, yet did Caroline occupy
my heart and thoughts, and, whenever I was
alone, I found they turned wholly on her;
but, as I dreaded the dangerous recollection, I took every poffible means to remove
it, and remained alone as feldom as poffible.
Manteul feldom left me; he found, each
day, his attachment increafe, and feemed
to fear we fhould part too foon. He told
me he had received letters from Drefden,
which

which had lain at his banker's, waiting his arrival at London, that gave him vaft pleafure. " My return," faid he, " may be much fooner than I fuppofed; but the event that will then call me back will be fo happy a one I fhall only have my friend to regret." I could eafily perceive he wifhed to open his heart to me, but that would have required a reciprocal confidence, and I was determined never to reveal my criminal fecret, nor ever once to pronounce the name of Caroline; I, therefore, forbore to afk him who the object of his attachment might be, or to put any one queftion which might lead him to fpeak.

" We had been prefented, by our ambaffador at London, to feveral Englifh noblemen; and, among others, we one day dined with the Earl of Salifbury. After dinner the toaft went round, as you know, Walftein, is the cuftom in England, and the health of the favourite lady given by each gueft. When the toaft came to me, my heart named Caroline, and the word rofe to my lips. I forbore, however, and begged they would excufe my naming the lady whofe health I drank. They joked me on my great difcretion, and drank to the health of the fair incognito.

" I fhall not be fo difcreet as Lindorf," faid Manteul, when it came to his turn; " I am proud to drink the health of Matilda, Countefs of Walftein."

" The name ftruck me fo forcibly that I fcarcely could believe what I heard real; but it was repeated round the table fo often that I could no longer doubt it was that fame Matilda by whom I had been fo tenderly

derly beloved, and whom I had fo cruelly offended., It is impoffible I fhould paint the agitation I was in; though, but a moment before, I fhould not have fuppofed any human power could have pronounced a name,, except Caroline, that might have made an equal impreffion. Manteul fat too far off for me to afk whether it was Matilda whom he loved; yet, how might I doubt when I beheld his animated countenance, as he repeated, himfelf, and heard others repeat, her name? I looked and thought him handfomer than ufual; he feemed to poffefs all the qualities of a lover, and, certainly, faid I, he is beloved. The letters which gave him fo much pleafure are; certainly, from Matilda, and his quick return to Drefden, which is to render him fo happy, is, alfo, as certainly, the confequence of her command : he is

M 2   then

then to receive her hand whofe heart he already poffeffes!

" Thefe ideas ran in my mind all the afternoon, .and accompanied me to the play, whither I was dragged in fpite of myfelf. I wifhed immediately to have con-verfed with Manteul, to have learned his fecret; reproached myfelf for having miffed the opportunity, and feared left it might not return; at laft, my thoughts were fo difturbed that, finding myfelf uneafy in the play-houfe, where I neither heard nor faw, I determined to quit it and come home. I there waited the arrival of Manteul with an impatience wholly unaccountable to my-felf. It was not long before he came; my going had alarmed him, and fcarcely did I give him time to tell me fo before I afked if the lady whofe health he had drunk

were

were the lady he loved, and if she were
sister to the Count of Walstein, Ambassa-
dor in Russia."

" Ay, certainly," replied he, with tranfport; " she, she herself, your charming
countrywoman! Are you acquainted with
her? It is some time since she left Berlin."

" I know her brother," replied I, elud-
ing his question. " The Count of Walstein has been to me more than a friend; a
father, a saviour, the man in the world most
dear to my heart."

" Ah! dear Lindorf," said Manteul,
embracing me with rapture, " if you are
upon these terms with the Count of Walstein, I may owe all my future bliss to
your friendship. She has often protested
M 3   that

that her brother, alone, had a right to dif-
pofe of her hand; and to him you may
fpeak for me; you may engage him to
favour my paffion.——Say, will you, Lindorf, will you?"

"Doubt it not, my friend. Should
Matilda, alfo, find this union that which
her heart defires, I then will ufe all the
power of my friendfhip with the Count to
engage him in your intereft. But I thought
Matilda, in fome meafure, contracted to
the Baron de Zaftrow."

"Alas! it was that projected marriage
which alone determined me to leave Drefden. I was the friend of de Zaftrow, and
would not become his rival. I, then, was
ignorant how much Matilda difliked him;
but the letter from my fifter, which I found
waiting

waiting my arrival here, informed me of it, and has given me the moſt flattering hopes."

" And had you none before you received that letter ?"

" None, none. Matilda never teſtified any thing more than eſteem for me, and that friendſhip which I thought the conſequence of her intimacy with my ſiſter ; ſhe did not ſeem even to perceive how much, I preferred her to every other woman. Before I left her I myſelf knew not the ſtrength of my own paſſion; but my ſiſter's letter, by making happineſs poſſible, has made me feel how much I adore that lovely lady."

" I moſt ardently wiſhed to get a ſight of this letter he mentioned, and my wiſh

was

was gratified; he gave it me to read.—
" Here, take it, my friend," faid he, " and
fee if I have not fome reafon to flatter myfelf I am beloved."—I accordingly took it
and, with great emotion, began to read.

" Mademoifelle de Manteul blamed her
" brother for departing, not following her
" advice, and openly paying his addreffes
" to the young Countefs. The Baron de
" Zaftrow had no right to be affronted;
" he was hated, and the marriage would
" never take place. Every thing, on the
" contrary, proved to her that her brother
" was beloved; fhe had remarked it before
" he left Drefden, and fhe now had not
" any doubt. Matilda was very forry
" when fhe heard he was gone, fhe had
" even fhed tears; her former cheerfulnefs
" had forfaken her, and what convinces
" me,

" me, faid fhe, your abfence caufes her me-
" lancholy is that it redoubles whenever
" England is mentioned. She yefterday
" faid, in a pet which made her look more
" lovely, " I wonder why the men are all
" fo eager to run to that good for nothing
" England!" This, brother, I fhould think
" a tolerably favourable fymptom, and, if
" you want a ftill ftronger, I muft tell you
" fhe herfelf has begged me to fhow her
" your letters. Profit by this informa-
" tion. You have ftill time enough to
" repair the folly you have committed in
" leaving Drefden. Write me a letter,
" immediately; not by way of anfwer to
" this, but feem to confide the fecret of
" your paffion for my young friend to me;
" entreat me to found her thoughts; fay
" fear alone occafioned you to go, but that
" the leaft ray of hope will bring you

" back;

" back; fhe will read the letter in my
" prefence: I fhall fee what impreffion it
" makes, and I dare believe the fecret of
" her heart will not efcape my penetration.
" I hope foon to give you more certain
" information which fhall haften your
" return."

" This letter feemed to me a clear proof
that Matilda loved young Manteul, and I
felt a painful fenfation, a fpafm of the heart,
which I could not account for, and which
I endeavoured to conceal. I returned the
letter, and confirmed his hopes.—" I have
written to my fifter," faid he, " exactly as
fhe prefcribed, and I impatiently wait her
anfwer: if, as fhe thinks, it fhould be favourable, and if Matilda will permit me to
afpire to the honour and happinefs of making her mine, you, dear Lindorf, may be

fer-

ferviceable to my interefts with the Count, her brother. I may owe my felicity to you, and my friendfhip for you will thus be increafed."

" This I folemnly promifed, but not without a fenfation that feemed very like jealoufy, which the defcription he gave of the lovely Matilda augmented. I could not deny I had often feen her before fhe left Berlin, and he added, " You would not know her, Lindorf; no, you would not know her. You cannot imagine how much fhe is altered, how much improved. I know not whether it be poffible to find a more beautiful woman; but a more graceful, a more charming one the world does not contain: fhe has every thing that can feduce and awe the heart. Her features have not a tame regularity; no, each has

M 6   an

an expreffion peculiar to itfelf; her countenance is continually varying, and is the
mirror of a moft excellent heart, and a
moft amiable mind. Never long the fame,
fhe is playful, fportive, froward, cheerful,
pretending to take pet, and laughing at the
deception fhe has occafioned. She infpires
joy and pleafure in all around her. At
other times, mild, fond, and full of fenfibility, fhe would melt the coldeft or the
hardeft heart. Such I beheld her, every
day; and how might I refift fo many al-
lurements; or what fhall be my happinefs
fhould fhe become mine?"

"My fecret regret for having wilfully
caft this happinefs from me was the anfwer
my heart returned to Manteul. And had
I!——had I been beloved by this charming
lady! And did it once depend only on me

to

to have made her for ever mine! Oh! how little had I merited a gift the value of which too late I knew! What! had she not a right to forget the man who repaid her affection with the blackeſt ingratitude; neglected, abandoned her, and, on the very firſt occaſion, yielding wholly to the love of another, repelled the heart which fondly had beſtowed itſelf on him, and obliged it to ſeek a mate more worthy?——Theſe ideas rapidly ſucceeded each other in my mind, and gave me an abſent and gloomy air, at which Manteul might well have been ſurpriſed; but he was too much intereſted in the ſubject of the converſation to perceive it; was too deſirous of continuing to ſpeak of his dear Matilda, and his future hopes. It was not poſſible, however, for me to hear him unmoved; I, therefore, pretended I was not very well, and withdrew.

" No

" No fooner was I alone than I began to inquire what my fenfations were, and how I might feel this ftrange emotion concerning an event which I ought to have forefeen. Since I had not loved Matilda, fince I had renounced her heart and hand, what were my rights? Ought I not to be happy that another had been more juft, and made reparation for my wrongs? Alas! fo far was I from being happy, from thinking thus, that it feemed as if Manteul bore away a treafure which appertained to me alone; nay, I was · inconfiftent, unjuft enough to accufe Matilda of want of conftancy, guilty as I myfelf had been! I recollected every circumftance of our acquaintance, thofe tender promifes, fo ingenuous, fo often repeated in her letters, to love me, and me only, and exclaimed all women are inconftant; as if I myfelf had

not

not been an example that men have, at least
that I had, very little reason for these reproaches !

" I next reflected on the situation in
which I stood with Manteul, and that folly
which, a second time, had made me the
rival of a friend. Yet durst I not allow
myself to say I was his rival, but promised,
if he were beloved, as every thing gave
me reason to suppose, I would serve him
with all the ardour of friendship : this I
presently assured him of, and we waited,
with equal impatience, the answer of his
sister, which was to contain his sentence."

" Well, but Caroline ? Is she wholly
forgotten ; already effaced from that heart
where she had reigned with such unbounded
sway ?"

" From

" From my own experience, Walſtein, I am convinced the heart, when it abſo-lutely loſes hope, loſes, in part, its pain; not, perhaps, in every inſtance, but in moſt; and, where love is the paſſion, whenever a new objeſt is found, that, by any concurrence of circumſtances, becomes intereſting, the former is preſently forgot-ten; at leaſt, ſo far forgotten as not to be remembered with the ſame reſtleſs and tor-menting ſenſations. I thought of Caroline, Counteſs of Walſtein, but not of Caroline of Lichtfield, and was moſt happy to en-courage the mutability; my imagination no longer wandered in the gardens of Rin-daw, or dwelt in the pavilion, but ſaw Ca-roline at Berlin, there in company with the beſt of huſbands, and enjoying her felicity. Happy was I when thus I might remem-ber her without remorſe, and, whenever

her

her name rofe to memory, the name of my
friend was, alfo, prefent; while that of Matilda, which Manteul was inceffantly re-
peating, gave me an emotion, the origin
of which I, who had had fo much experience, could not miftake. Thus, my
friend, you fee my cure is far advanced;
and you foon will learn in what manner I
was perfectly reftored.

" On our firft arrival in England, we
defigned to have travelled through the different counties; but, fuppofing we fhould
remain there all winter, intended to have
deferred our journey till the fpring. Manteul, determined to depart immediately,
fhould his fifter's letter recall him to Drefden, entreated me now to go with him and,
at leaft, vifit the moft famous places.
Since I had learned his fecret I was ill at
eafe,

eafe, and little inclined to reft long in one
place. A journey, I imagined, would be
fome relief, and I willingly confented. We
fet off, therefore, paffed through various
counties, and a part of Wales, ftopping
to examine what was held moft curious and
interefting. This, dear Count, is not the
moment to give you a defcription of a
country where peace and liberty produce
abundance, where the productive fields,
cultivated by wealthy farmers, are not,
like ours, the fcenes of bloody battles, and
all their direful attendants. Certain of
finding them nourifhment, the inhabitants
fear not to marry and beget children. The
towns, villages, and cities, are extremely
populous, and every perfon feems happy;
and, as the Englifh nobility pafs one part
of the year at their country feats, where
they contribute to the profperity of their
tenants,

tenants, thofe beautiful country feats are built with an elegance, and preferved in a ftyle of grandeur and tafte, very different from the gloomy magnificence of our antique chateaus. If we wifh to form an idea of the beauties of nature, and the inexpreffible charms of a country life, we muft go to England."

" You augment the wifh I have to fee that country," faid the Count; " I intend to take my dear Caroline thither; but, till that happens, fhall be glad of farther information."

" I know not whether I am capable of affording you any," replied Lindorf, " for we travelled with too much rapidity, and our hearts and minds were too much preoccupied, to remark the numerous things deferving

deferving notice. I have only juft mentioned what muft neceffarily ftrike every
foreigner who beholds England for the firft
time.

" Impatience to receive news from Drefden made us foon turn our faces towards
London: I certainly was more uneafy
than Manteul. The hope he had conceived contributed much to his happinefs,
which I rather envied than participated;
and the more cheerful and animated I faw
him the more did my fecret chagrin and
gloom increafe. I fpoke to him, however,
continually, concerning Matilda, led him
to repeat the moft minute circumftances,
and was as inexhauftible in my queftions
as Manteul was in replies. This was our
chief fubject of converfation, and, every
moment, grief, regret, jealoufy, and I
may add love, acquired new force. Man-
                                    teul

teul found no letters when we came to London; but, two days after our arrival, as I was rifing, intending to breakfaft with him, his fervant brought me a letter, with my addrefs. Surprifed at this, I immediately was going to him, but was informed he was gone out, and would not be home before dinner. My aftonifh-ment increafed, and I opened the letter, not without emotion, which ftill became more forcible when I faw the cover inclof-ed a letter that had been opened, addreffed to Manteul, with the poft-mark of Dref-den, which, by its fize, feemed ftill to contain another. This I fuppofed to be the anfwer of his fifter, and a letter in-clofed from Matilda. But wherefore not bring them himfelf ? In fpite of my impa-tience to fee it, I began by reading the few lines Manteul had written in the cover.

"" Here

" Here it is," faid Lindorf, taking it from his pocket-book, " and imagine what was my furprife."

" I know not whether to the beft of
" friends or moft traiterous of men I
" inclofe the letters I have juft received;
" while I thus abfolutely cede to the for-
" mer opinion, I fhall prove I wifh to find
" I am not miftaken, however appearances
" may fay the contrary.—And is Lindorf
" then the lover of Matilda? By her be-
" loved? The hufband of her choice, fe-
" lected by her brother, and acknowledg-
" ed by her heart? The man to whom fhe
" would inftantly facrifice the homage of
" the adoring world; and is it from her-
" felf I learn all this?—Oh! Lindorf,
" what motive can you have had for the
" inconceivable myfterioufnefs of your
                                    " conduct?

" conduct? I cannot think you capable of
" bafe treachery; yet I had fome right to
" your confidence and fincerity.—I am
" loft in doubt, and own I fear the confe-
" quences of meeting you at this moment.
" Send your anfwer to the Orange Coffee-
" houfe; there can be no reafon for longer
" diffimulation, for, fince you are beloved,
" you no longer have a rival.

" Manteul."

" It is impoffible to tell you what I felt.
Was I—Was I ftill beloved by the charming, the conftant Matilda? Was it for me,
ungrateful as I was, that fhe refufed the
addreffes of de Zaftrow, of Manteul, nay
of *the whole world!* I opened the letter
and found one addreffed to me; the hand
was well known, and an emotion, almoft
involuntary, brought it to my lips. I was

about

about to open and enjoy the excefs of my happinefs when a fudden and bitter re-flection ftopped me. Again at the expence of a friend muft I be happy; and this friend had reafon to fuppofe me perfidious. I could not endure the thought. You, dear Count, are capable of imagining what my feelings were, and the increafe they fuffered by recollection. This was the fecond time love had affaulted friendfhip, and a fecond time was I defirous friendfhip fhould be victorious. I would not read the letters till I firft had juftified myfelf to Manteul, and till I had his free confent to read them: I locked them up, and inftant-ly went in fearch of him to the coffee-houfe, where he had not yet been, and where the moft probable way of meeting him would have been to wait; but waiting at this moment was impoffible. I ran to feek

him

him elfewhere. I rather chofe fpeaking to
him than writing a letter long enough to
have explained all the reafons of my conduct, which little fuited my impatience;
but, as we might mifs each other in the
fearch, I left a line at the coffee-houfe,
faying "he did me juftice in believing me
" incapable of perfidy; that, certainly, I
" had many things to reproach myfelf with,
" but not that of treachery towards him.
" Matilda only had a right to complain. I
" begged him to wait at the coffee-houfe,
" and pledged myfelf to give him every ex-
" planation he could require, affuring him I
" fhould not take a moment's reft till he
" had heard me. I had not read, nor would
" read, a line in the letters he had fent me,
" and hoped to prove how highly I valued
" his efteem and friendfhip!"

After giving this note to the waiter I continued my search, went to the Pruffian Ambaffador's, into the Park, to all our acquaintances, but miffed him every where; and, returning to the coffee-houfe, found, to my great vexation, he had been there and was gone, but that he had left a note for me, which was this. (Lindorf read it to the Count.)

"I wifh to fee and fpeak with you, dear " Lindorf, but it is not poffible. Lord " Cavendifh has requefted me to accom-- " pany him to Newmarket; he is fetting " off immediately, and I fcarcely have time " to write a word. You know how defir- " ous I am of feeing thofe famous races, " and I was the more ready to accept the " offer becaufe my mind is at prefent in " great need of relief. Your note, and " efpecially your eagernefs to fee me before
                                          " you

" you have read your letters, tell me all that
" I at prefent wifh to know. Read them,
" dear friend, and if you are not, in half
" an hour, on the road to Drefden you do not
" merit your happinefs. Could any thing
" difturb, or alter, my efteem and friend-
" fhip for you it would be to hear you were
" in London at this time to-morrow. Fare-
" well, dear Lindorf, and be as happy as
" you deferve; as happy as you muft be
" with the moft lovely of women. I will
" feek another like her, if poffible, and whofe
" heart is free. Should the company and
" fports of Newmarket have the effect
" I hope, you will foon hear from me. I
" doubt not but you will write and give
" me the account you promife; not by way
" of explanation, it is not requifite, but in
" the confidence of friendfhip, and to one
" who is infinitely interefted both for Lin-

" dorf

" dorf and Matilda. *She*, you fay, *only has*
" *a right to complain*—Happy Lindorf!—
" Fly, behold her, and fhe will not have
" that right long.

" Manteul."

" Scarcely had I finifhed before I flew to
the houfe of Lord Cavendifh, hoping ftill to
find him, but they were gone poft, and
I hefitated, for a moment, whether I fhould
or fhould not follow; but motives fo ftrong
and a defire fo ardent drew me elfewhere
that I could not long refift. I once more
read the note of Manteul, and finding he
avoided me, " Why," faid I, " fhould I
force the fight of a happy rival on him in the
firft paroxyfm of grief?" Was I in reality
beloved by the generous Matilda? Manteul, only, yet, had told me fo, and I
longed to fee the confirmation. I, therefore, returned home, and read the two letters

ters I am going to fhew you. You will
begin by reading that of Mademoifelle de
Manteul, as I did, though moft impatient
to fee the other, which, addreffed to me,
made my heart palpitate. I trembled
to open a paper where each word, traced
by the hand of Matilda, muft be a reproach to this inconftant heart. She, perhaps, knew not my infidelity; but was I,
therefore, lefs culpable?—Ah! when I did
read, how did her ingenuous and affectionate foul, which infufed itfelf into the paper,
augment my wrongs, and make me more
felf-odious! " I began with this," faid
Lindorf, giving it to the Count.

" Mademoifelle de Manteul firft afked a
" thoufand pardons of her brother for hav-
" ing given him falfe hopes. Deceived her-
" felf, fhe had believed the thing fhe

" wifhed

" wifhed to be was true, and that he had
" been the fecret object of Matilda's love. It
" was your letter," added fhe, " that very
" letter I requefted you to write, and from
" which I expected effects fo very differ-
" ent, that deftroyed all my hopes. No,
" brother, you are not the beloved man.
" Matilda has long fince yielded her heart.
" She refufes the homage of de Zaftrow,
" of you, and of the whole world, for the
" fake of your new friend, that very Ba-
" ron of Lindorf of whom you fpeak. She
" faw but his name in your letter and, in-
" ftantly, her fecret was betrayed: yet it
" can now be no fecret to you, for, being
" thus intimate with that gentleman, he,
" by this, has, certainly, made you his con-
" fidant; certainly, has told you he has
" long fince been contracted to the young
" Countefs of Walftein." Her brother, the

" moft

" moſt intimate friend of Lindorf, pro-
" moted this union, and their hearts were
" accordant to his wiſhes. Matilda declares
" nothing can diſſolve this contract but
" death; for, though Lindorf ſhould even
" prove inconſtant, ſhe never will.   Your
" paſſion, therefore, dear brother, for your
" own ſake, you will vanquiſh, and I think
" I know you to be ſufficiently reaſonable
" and generous to reſt aſſured it will change
" to friendſhip, and that you will take a
" pleaſure at once to ſerve Matilda and her
" lover.   This you may do by giving him
" the incloſed letter, which the poor young
" lady had no means of ſending.   It is not
" ſhe that requeſts this, but I; thinking
" it the beſt means of effecting your cure.
" Tell this Lover that his miſtreſs is per-
" ſecuted by her aunt, who will oblige her
" to wed de Zaſtrow, whom ſhe hates; that

" this

" this will certainly occafion her death;
" prevail on him to depart inftantly, that
" he may confole, deliver, and carry her
" off, if neceffary; and, indeed, I fee no
" other means. What can he have to fear,
" fince he is authorized by her brother?
" You well may fuppofe, Charles, I fhould
" have been happy had you been the man;
" but her heart was beftowed before fhe
" came to Drefden. Endeavour, there-
" fore, only to contribute to her happinefs;
" and, perhaps, to your fifter's likewife."

This latter phrafe, which had efcaped
the obfervation of Lindorf, made the Count
fmile, and confirmed him in his former
opinion of Mademoifelle de Manteul. He
returned the letter to Lindorf, who then
gave him that from Matilda—" Read,"
faid he, " and think what muft have been
the impreffion it made on me!"

" Drefden—

- " Dresden————Yes, M. Lindorf, Ma-
" tilda writes to you. Your friend, Ma-
" tilda. She does very wrong, to be sure;
" she ought not to be the first to break this
" excellent silence. Oh ! yes, yes; I know
" I do wrong ; but, I likewise know, I can-
" not help it. There are certain moments
" in life when the heart speaks louder than
" reason, and compels it to silence, and
" my heart says so many many things that
" I am obliged to listen and do whatever
" it pleases. It tells me, for example, I
" shall be less unhappy when I have relat-
" ed all my sufferings to my friend ; and I
" already feel it tells me truth. Since I
" have begun to write it seems as if my
" griefs were all changed into so many
" pleasures ; but, alas ! these will presently
" vanish ; and no sooner will my letter be
" ended than my torments will re-com-

N 5   " mence.

" mence. My brother ftill in Ruffia, Lin-
" dorf ftill in England, de Zaftrow ftill at
" Drefden, and poor Matilda ftill perfe-
" cuted——My aunt requires impoffibi-
" lities. Have I two hearts that I may
" beftow one on de Zaftrow? And if I had
" a thoufand, fhould not I give them all
" to—— to——. Ever fince I have begun
" to write this letter, nay, ever fince I firft
" thought of writing it, have I been in-
" ceffantly torturing my imagination for
" the beft manner of telling you what I
" feel, and how I might fay all I have to
" fay; but the more I think the lefs I fuc-
" ceed. It will be impoffible you fhould
" underftand me—— I will think no more
" on the matter; I will fuffer my hand and
" my heart to go their own way. I re-
" quire fincerity, and have a right to give
" the example——Yes, M. Lindorf (fee!
                                    " fee!

" fee! I am ftill thinking about the man-
" ner). Well then, dear, dear Lindorf!, I
" love you, and fhall love you as long as I
" live!—And, be affured, I will live and
" die either Matilda Walftein or Matilda
" Lindorf.——Do not be terrified at this
" my eternal conftancy. No, dear Lin-
" dorf, it does not entail itfelf on *you*:
" far am I from fuppofing you under the
" fame obligation. With myfelf only, not
" with you, have I entered into this en-
" gagement. I have heard men, may
" change as often as they pleafe, without
" becoming lefs eftimable in their own
" eyes, or even in the eyes of the women;
" and it muft be true, fince my brother, the
" wifeft and the beft of men, has changed,
" nobody knows why, and feems no longer
" to love his poor fifter.——Ah! Lindorf,
" dear Lindorf, do you fupply the place
" of

"of this brother, who forfakes me; he is
"fo far off I have no means of reclaiming
"his friendfhip; but, certainly, yours,
"Lindorf, will come to my aid. Advife,
"tell me, how I may avoid a marriage I
" deteft; preferve me for,——Alas! if not
"for Lindorf, for myfelf.——If it be true
" he loves another——I afk no queftions,
"I fhall know it foon enough; yet it will
" not alter my prefent manner of thinking,
" neither with refpect to you, the Baron de
" Zaftrow, nor all the men on earth, for
" never among them all will I chufe more
" than one. This I know, and what far-
" ther knowledge do I want? Only tell me
" you will remain the friend of Matilda;
" the word *friend* will afcertain your fince-
" rity; which will be ftill farther confirmed
" by your franknefs, and eagernefs to an-
" fwer this, to relieve me from the cruel in-
" quietude your filence, that of my bro-
" ther,

" ther, and the absence of you both occa-
" fion; from that neglect which resembles
" offence, forgetfulness, and death, and
" which certainly will be death, if it con-
" tinue much longer, to Matilda Wal-
" ftein.

" P. S. I know not how to direct this
" letter, nor where to fend it. Alas! I
" know not whether you or my brother
" neglect me the moft; but you both
" are ——— What in the world I love the
" beft! Which, I am afraid, is as much as
" to fay, ungrateful."

The Count was affected at reading this
letter, and feverely reprehended himfelf for
having fuffered his paffion for Caroline to
make him fo far forget his fifter. He
ought not to have been fatisfied with writing a letter; he fhould have fuppofed it
might be intercepted, and have gone himfelf.

felf. He began to imagine he, only, was in the wrong.——" You may think," faid Lindorf, ", what I felt from what you your-felf feel."—The Count was going to give back the letter.——" No, keep it," faid Lindorf, " and, if ever I fhould be wretch-ed enough to forget it, or give my Ma-tilda a moment's grief, fhew me but that letter again and I fhall inftantly repair the wrong."

" I did not hefitate a moment, after I had read it," continued he, " concerning how I muft act. To fly to her, to confole her, to intreat her to forgive the injuries I had done her, to tear her from the arms of tyranny, and dedicate my life to her happinefs, was the firft wifh, the vow, of my heart. I clearly faw they deceived her, fince fhe ftill fup-pofed you in Ruffia. They, no doubt, had intercepted your letters; fhe was befet

with

with snares, and by people devoted to de Zaftrow. The danger was so preffing that I determined immediately to depart; the recollection of Manteul only could have prevented me, and this his note counteracted. *Could any thing difturb, or alter, my efteem and friendfhip for you it would be to hear you were in London at this time to-morrow.* I determined, however, not to leave England till I had removed every doubt refpecting my own conduct, and the myftery I had made of my engagements with Matilda. I, therefore, fat down and wrote a circumftantial account of what my motives and intentions were, in which I concealed nothing but the name of Caroline, and owned that what he had faid of Matilda had more than revived my former inclination for her; but that, feeling fhe had every right to forget me, I had refolved

to make her every reparation I might, by
aiding her in this her fuppofed new paffion.
My letter was long, and 1 was ftill writing
when the fervant, whom Manteul had
taken with him, returned. He, on recollection, had fent him back with another
note, which was but a fort of repetition of
the preceding one, fearing left it had not
come to hand, and that my departure was
by that means deferred. He added new
and ftronger motives to haften me, and,
that I might not have the leaft uneafinefs
on his account, affured me, " He looked
" on it as a lucky event. Too young, at
" prefent, to marry (he is not twenty) no
" woman but Matilda could have excufed
" his entering into the marriage ftate. The
" fufpicion of being beloved by her had
" led him wild, but the conviction of the
" contrary had reftored him to reafon and
" liberty. By thefe he would profit, would
                            " ftudy,

" ftudy, and travel for fome years, and
" hoped, when we met again, to find me
" the happy hufband of the moft lovely of
" women. Whatever my reafons might
" have been for forfaking her, he was cer-
" tain I no longer fhould be inconftant the
" moment I faw her. He knew me too
" well to believe I fhould not immediately
" fly to her affiftance, though it were but
" from motives of friendfhip, and if I even
" were incapable of love. He concluded
" by telling me his fervant had orders to
" return to him as foon as he had feen me
" get into the poft-chaife."

" I fent back the voluminous letter I
had written, and his fervant departed for
Newmarket, at the fame time that I left
London. The wind was favourable, and
we had a quick paffage. I found Varner
at Hamburg, where he had been feveral
weeks,

weeks, detained by contrary winds, and at which he had been much afflicted. He gave me your short note, and my banker, the same day, delivered the succeeding letter; both were equally pressing, both requested my immediate return, without explaining your motives. Of this there was no need; the request of Walstein need not fear disobedience, and, had I not been returning, I instantly should have set out. Yet how must I confess that my heart made me take the road to Dresden instead of that to Berlin! I have no excuse unless it were a *presentiment*. I endeavoured to persuade myself that a few days delay could not give you any pain, though it might be of the utmost consequence to Matilda. I was anxious to see her, to persuade her to come with me, and bring her to her brother. Nay, I even interpreted your two so pressing

sing

fing letters into pofitive orders that related
folely to Matilda, and concluded I beft was
anfwering your intentions by flying to her
aid before I faw you. I therefore ftopped
only at Hamburg till good horfes and equi-
page could be found. The reft you know;
my rencontre with de Zaftrow, and my
furprife at feeing Matilda leap out of the
poft-chaife. Though I have not yet ven-
tured to tell you, before her; how much the
alteration in her perfon affected, aftonifhed,
and enchanted me; how fuperior fhe was
to the Matilda I had formerly known, to
her Manteul had defcribed, or, even, to
what my imagination had fuppofed. Oh!
Walftein, how beauteous! how angelic did
fhe feem, embellifhed as her countenance
was by the emotions of her heart! The firft
words fhe uttered had fomething of tendernefs, of feeling, of foul, which it is impoffible

poffible to convey. I fee her now fly from the carriage, run with open arms, and hear her utter, "Lindorf, dear Lindorf, they want to fteal your Matilda from you, who is, and only will be, yours!"

"Her native innocence is above all fuf-picion; fhe loves, herfelf, and thinks it moft certain fhe is, herfelf, beloved. Not a year's filence, not all that others have faid, nor all that I have done, could fhake her conftancy. The moment fhe fees me they are all forgotten, and not a fhadow of doubt remains. Ah! when fainting and feeble fhe funk into my arms, pale, inanimate, and with half clofed eyes, how interefting was it to my foul! With what ardour did I fwear to live for her, and her alone! On her lips, as I bore her into the houfe, I pronounced the vow which I never can forget, no more than I can the raptu-rous fenfations I that moment experienced.

"My

" My affair with de Zaſtrow, my wound,
the tender care ſhe has taken of me, her
underſtanding, her grace, her ingenuous
mind, all have augmented my paſſion.
Yet will I own I felt ſome emotion at the
ſight of Caroline; but it was of a very
different kind from what I had formerly
known. I ſaw with pleaſure, yes, Walſtein, with infinite pleaſure, you were beloved, and Caroline was to me as a ſiſter,
the wife of my friend and brother. And
now, dear Count, you know my inmoſt
heart, and, I hope, will not delay to beſtow the happineſs I ſo ardently deſire,
which preſent conviction tells me I deſerve,
and which will make felicity perfect."

" My felicity," replied the Count, tenderly embracing him, " will not be perfect
till I behold Matilda and Lindorf as happy
as I myſelf am; nor ſhall it be long before

fore thefe new bonds of affinity and friendfhip fhall be formed, which will leave me
nothing farther to wifh."

Walftein, then, related all his paft fcenes
with Caroline. Lindorf fhuddered at the
idea of the divorce. " Good God!" faid he,
" could you fuppofe 1 would be acceffary
to fuch a facrifice! That I would be happy
at the expence of Walftein!"

" It was the happinefs of Caroline that
was in conteft, and neither thou nor I,
Lindorf, ought then to recede. The letters I wrote, and which thou wouldeft have
found on thy arrival, would have removed
every fcruple: friendfhip and delicacy
muft have yielded to motives more deci-
five. My reafons were good, and my
meafures well taken, and thou couldeft not
but have acted accordingly."

" Afk me not how I fhould have acted,"
replied

replied Lindorf; " I, fortunately, have not been put to the proof. I am proud of being your brother. You only could de- ferve Caroline, and fhe alone could equal your virtues. Matilda, perhaps, is, by temper and nature, better fuited to your friend Lindorf."

" She does not know," faid the Count, " that Caroline has been her rival?" " She knows every thing," replied Lindorf, with vivacity. " She has a right to know every thing. My heart were unworthy of her had I any fecrets. In juftice, I was oblig- ed to account for my coolnefs, my filence, my voyage to England. Might I deceive her? No, impoffible; and, had I even fo intended, no fuch intention could have been kept. Her noble franknefs, her open candour, would irrefiftibly have enfured like confidence and like fincerity. No fooner

were

were we alone in the poſt-chaiſe than ſhe
ſpoke of you and your marriage; and aſked if I knew her ſiſter. A full confeſſion
of all that ,had paſſed was my anſwer;
and, far from feeling jealouſy or vexation,
I found, as I ſpoke, ſhe became attached
to Caroline, was deſirous of her friendſhip, and determined to imitate her beſt
qualities and virtues. " Oh! how dearly," ſaid ſhe, " ſhall I love this charming
Caroline! How happy will ſhe make my
brother! And how gladly ſhall I learn,
from her, to reclaim and fix my rover,
my Lindorf!"—Since Matilda has ſeen
her, ſhe has told me, with a tone of ſince-
rity that leaves no doubt on the mind,
" Ah! Lindorf, how perfectly are you
juſtified in your paſſion! I never could
have pardoned you had you ſeen Caroline
with indifference!" Such, dear Count, is
your

your fifter; and judge whether I ought not to adore her."

Arrived at Berlin, the firft care of the Count was to prefent his friend and fifter to the King, and requeft his approbation of their marriage; which obtained, the happy family went to the Walftein eftate, where Caroline had fled *from* her hufband, on the bridal day, and *to* him, on the morning of the projected divorce, and of which Juftin was fteward. There, in the Count's chapel, was the marriage celebrated, without other witneffes than Walftein, Caroline, the tenants of the Chateau, and fome of the villagers. As they left the church, Louifa came to pay her refpects to Lindorf, to whom fhe was prefented by Caroline. He beheld both thefe lovely women, who formerly had raifed fuch commotions in his breaft, with perfect tranquillity; and, preffing the hand of the Count who ſtood next him, " I feel, at this moment," ſaid he, " I am worthy to be the brother of Walſtein. I was diſtracted for Louiſa, Caroline I adored, but Matilda I love, and ſhall for ever love !"

The CONCLUSION.

'To thoſe who wiſh to be informed of every thing that paſſes we ſhall further ſay, that Lindorf continued thus to think; that he made his lovely lady happy, attained to the higheſt rank in the army, and diſtinguiſhed himſelf on ſeveral occaſions. That Edmund, Count of Walſtein, was a pillar to the throne, a friend of the King, a protector of the people, a ſupporter of the wretched, and that he found, in the conſtant affection of his dear Caroline, and

the

the good conduct of his children, the full recompenfe of his virtues; while Caroline, the adored, the beloved Caroline, meeting the admiration fhe merited, was the happieft as fhe was the moft angelic of women.

We fhall likewife add that the young Baron de Zaftrow, admiring his Parifian graces, engrafted on a German trunk, finding he pleafed only Mademoifelle de Manteul, who pleafed not him, returned to Paris and his gaming friends, purfued his theatrical conquefts, and made fuch good ufe of his time, money, and conftitution that, in lefs than a year, he was ruined, difeafed, and dead. His aunt, perceiving Matilda had had good reafon for her refufal, pardoned, and left her all her wealth.

- Mademoifelle de Manteul retired, at firft, into a convent; after which fhe obtained the place of a Maid of Honour, at court;

court; where, exercifing that fpirit of intrigue with which fhe was fo liberally endowed, fhe became perfectly competent to her poft.

Her young brother, the well difpofed and amiable Manteul, for whom we have been interefted, and whom we faw fet off to Newmarket, met with Lady Sophia Seymour, who was coufin german to the Count and Matilda, and who greatly refembled the latter. Manteul now found he was far from having fuffered a lofs, inafmuch as Lady Sophia, no-wife inferior to her lovely coufin, loved him with all the ardour with which Matilda loved Lindorf. The Count, in a voyage he made to London, in company with Caroline, had the pleafure of forming this union, and making two more lovers happy.

THE END.